ROBERT E. LEE

OF

COLORADO

A STORY OF
A MAN WHO DID MAKE
A DIFFERENCE

By
Joe Shoemaker

with
Bill Miller

A. B. Hirschfeld Press

ACKNOWLEDGMENTS

Numerous individuals helped contribute to this book:

Liz Andrews; Chuck Cordt, Washburn University; Terry Gilberto; Helen Johnson; Ginny Miller; Jerry Nix; Carl Nordstrom; Thayne Swenson; Joan Barker, Topeka High School History Society; and Bob Lee's family and friends.

CONTENTS

FOREWORD

Bill Daniels

Robert E. Lee, only known as Bob Lee, was an exceptional citizen in the great nation in which we live. His priorities were his family, his country, the Republican Party and his job. In all of the some thirty-six years that I worked with Bob as a fundraiser, as National Committeeman, as a candidate for Governor and associated with my company, I have never known a guy or gal as dedicated as Bob was to whatever his mission was. In addition, I know of no other person who worked more years, more months and more days at no pay for causes that he believed in. Put simply, Bobby's work for a cause was always 100% full speed all of the time. Republican politicians both elected and running for office used Bob as a sounding board. I know of no case where he gave them bad advice.

He believed that a political party started from the ground up and not the top down. To win an election, Bob would concentrate on the committeeman or committeewoman in a precinct, then move up to the district captains, and then to the county chairman, then the local officials, county officials, state officials, and all of the time he was trying to raise money for candidates. Bobby's only tools while he was working were a yellow pad (usually beat up and crinkled) and a couple pencils and more phone numbers than I knew anyone could possibly possess. He loved every minute of it.

Bob ended up working for our company full time, and what a pleasure it was to have him not only for myself but for all those in the company who loved Bobby. He was a very humble guy, not a braggart by any means unless he was talking about his days as an athlete. In later years, even a few years before he died, he was one tough competitor on the tennis court. But most of all, once Bob became your friend, you were locked in for life. He was a lovely, lovely man and a true gentleman.

I find it a great challenge to explain how much I deeply loved this man. This book will be treasured by everyone who reads it.

Robert E. Lee

ROBERT E. LEE – AN OVERVIEW

March 15, 1914 - July 3, 1998

As a real estate professional, Robert E. Lee knew the three most important words in determining the value of a piece of real estate were "location, location, location."

As a political strategist, Robert E. Lee believed that the three key words for a successful political campaign were "fundamentals, fundamentals, fundamentals." And the key fundamental in a political campaign, in Lee's strategy, was the neighborhood worker.

His idea of a perfect campaign was to have a knowledgeable, hard working neighborhood representative in every block. Once the "block worker" program was in place and functioning, Lee believed he could pick any block and have a good idea of how residents of that block would vote in the election. By having this information from all blocks he would have an excellent feeling on how the election would go.

While this book is about Robert E. Lee, political strategist, it is also about Robert E. Lee – father, athlete, businessman and patriot.

The patriot description came from John M. King, former Denver oil man, entrepreneur and Republican stalwart, whose financial empire crashed in the early 1970's. Lee was vice president of public affairs for Imperial-American Management Company, one of King's companies, in 1969.

"You should describe Bob as a patriot," King said. "He believed that good citizens had an obligation of participating in the process and helping those they believed in be elected. He never made a nickel out of politics. In fact, he was rather a poor man and had many financial difficulties because he spent so much of his time helping others. He spent his life in the shadows of other men whom he believed in and whom he helped get elected."

Ralph Clark, a close friend and fellow GOP official and party office holder, echoed this sentiment. "He never, ever tried to feather his own nest," Clark said. "He was enormously unselfish."

This book, then, is about a man who made a difference in the lives of not only people he helped to elect to high office, but to party people in the trenches. They, like him, gave of their time and money because they believed in the principles of the Republican Party.

Even more, they believed in the political process, particularly at a grass roots level, which distinguishes the American system from others throughout the world - and makes it work. Citizen participation.

Robert E. Lee was born in Topeka, Kansas on March 15, 1914. He grew up in Topeka and attended grade and high school and college there. He excelled in both athletics and student activities in high school and starred in three sports at Washburn College. As quarterback of his college football team, Bob learned that it took strong, confident, dedicated people in the front line to make the offense click. In politics, he believed that people made the difference. And it was on this fundamental belief that he built political organizations. He was totally unselfish - always deferring to others, giving the workers the credit. They were the ones, Bob believed, who made the difference between a winning and losing campaign.

Nevertheless, in every campaign Bob headed, two people recognized his political genius - the candidate he was working for, and the candidate he was against.

Bob met Elizabeth (Bee) Johnston on the Washburn campus. They were married in 1939. This marriage of 59 years, and the three children of the union, competed for Bob's love and attention with politics and sports. Bee, with a wry grin, commented, "I sometimes think politics won."

In 1940 the couple moved to Denver, Bee's home town and Bob entered the real estate business with his father-in-law, Earl Johnston, a real estate broker who had offices at 280 S. Downing Street.

When the United States entered World War II in 1941, even though he was 27 years of age, Bob felt obligated to become directly involved in the war effort. (He had abandoned the real estate business temporarily to work for Peter Kiewit & Sons, a Nebraska defense contractor.) He enlisted in the Navy in 1943, even though he was almost 30 years of age and the father of two children. He spent a year and a half on Guam, returning to Denver in December of 1945.

In Denver, a next door neighbor who was an officer in the Republican Party started talking to him about politics in Denver and Colorado. Bob became active in the Party. He expressed concern about "big government, the dangers of socialism and high taxes."

His political baptism of fire came in 1952 when he became involved in the 1952 Presidential campaign. He followed the lead of Colorado's Republican Senator Eugene Milliken and supported Senator Robert Taft, a conservative from Ohio, for the Republican nomination. The political wisdom of the time believed that Senator Milliken could deliver Colorado's 17 delegates to Senator Taft and Lee agreed. But a young State Senator, Will Nicholson, retired Brigadier General, figured otherwise. He produced 14 of 17 votes for Eisenhower and Lee experienced the pain of seeing his favored candidate defeated.

Leaders in the Republican Party and Eisenhower supporters urged Bob to forget and forgive - which he did. In 1955 Bob became an area leader for Will Nicholson in his successful campaign that produced that rarity of political creatures, a Republican mayor of Denver.

Nicholson ran behind the popular Democratic District Attorney, Bert Keating, throughout the campaign. It was during this campaign that Bob started perfecting his block worker organizational strategy. As an area leader, he was responsible for three political districts. Twenty of the precincts in two of the districts, which he knew were going to be strong for Nicholson, were among the last to report their tallies and they carried Nicholson to a sensational come from behind win over Keating.

During this campaign Bob met many of the people who became an important part of his personal and political life. He was elected Denver County Republican Chairman in 1958 and put his block worker organization to work to elect Richard Batterton as Nicholson's successor as Mayor of Denver.

Lee's political choices for office were not always successful. He was a strong Barry Goldwater supporter in the 1964 presidential election and saw incumbent Mayor Dick Batterton lose to Tom Currigan in the mayoral election of 1963. But he had major, major successes. He worked with other GOP county officials in metropolitan Denver counties and organized to get Jean Tool elected Colorado GOP chairman. Bob then led Colorado Republicans to one of the greatest political upsets in Colorado's history, the defeat in 1962 of highly respected Democratic Governor Steve McNichols by a then unknown Republican candidate, John Love of Colorado Springs.

This victory, in addition to his involvement in national presidential conventions, brought him to the attention of Republican leaders in Washington and throughout the country. The national party organization requested that he take his skills to New Jersey to help organize the campaign of C. Robert Sarcone, a Republican candidate for the New Jersey Senate. The organization he put together elected the Republican Sarcone running in a predominately Democratic district to the New Jersey Senate, allowing the GOP to maintain control of that body. It proved that Republicans, properly organized, could win in Eastern industrial states.

He created another political miracle in Florida in 1966 - the election of the first Republican governor in that southern state in 93 years. Like Governor Love in Colorado, Claude M. Kirk came out of political no man's land to win the Republican nomination and the governorship of the state. This gubernatorial victory in the South was extremely important for the presidential campaign of Richard Nixon in 1968. Bob not only played a part in that campaign but also recruited then State Senator Bill Armstrong to be Colorado campaign manager for Nixon.

Armstrong, then a 28-year old youngster in the Colorado Senate, later was elected to the United States Congress and the United States Senate.

"I learned a lot from watching Bob in action," Armstrong said. "Bob told me if you want to get somebody's support, you don't just ask them for that support, you ask them to do something and report back, and give them a specific job. That's how you really get them to feel they are a part of the action. It's getting them to do something very specific."

Bob suffered a severe heart attack shortly after the Kirk campaign and was hospitalized in Florida, preventing him from fully participating in setting up Kirk's gubernatorial staff and other political appointments.

But the health problem didn't slow him up for long. He became a close advisor to Richard Nixon and helped recruit delegates for Nixon from Colorado, New Jersey, Florida and Alaska (where son Eric was teaching school) to the Miami convention.

Back in Denver, he immediately became involved in the Denver School Board "anti-busing" campaign of 1969. His advice to the GOP candidates Frank Southworth and James Perrill – "Introduce yourself to voters. Tell them who you are and that you are against forced busing." Both won handily.

Perhaps Lee's most discouraging political campaign occurred in 1974, following Nixon's reelection in 1972. This was the year of a Republican primary for governor of Colorado, pitting Bill Daniels, a long time Republican financial supporter, cable television innovator and friend of Lee's, against John Vanderhoof, the incumbent. "Johnny Van," a shrewd and popular politician from Colorado's Western Slope, had succeeded to the governor's office when John Love resigned and accepted a job in Washington, D.C. as President Nixon's energy head.

In the mid-1970's, Lee left his beloved Colorado and organizational politics to accept an appointment from President Ford in Washington, D.C. to the Foreign Claims Commission. He returned to Colorado in 1978 and soon was embroiled in Republican politics once again.

In 1980 he accepted an appointment by the Chief Justice of the Colorado Supreme Court, Paul Hodges, to be Chairman of the 1980 Reapportionment Commission, established by a 1978 Constitutional Amendment. Chairing this Commission, composed of six Republicans and five Democrats, tested all the management and political skills Lee had acquired during his years of political activity. The final report was adopted unanimously by both the Colorado House and Senate.

In later years, Bob was associated with Daniels and Associates, one of the happiest periods of his life. He was a great admirer of Bill Daniels. In a 1995 letter to Daniels, Bob told Bill: "It is impossible to say everything I think about you. I'll sum it up by saying I've never known anyone that I respect or admire more than you." This explains why the Foreword to this book is written by Daniels.

In the following chapters, the life of Bob Lee, a man who truly made a difference, will be examined in depth.

Lee's philosophy was crystallized by his son, Eric: "He believed in fundamentals. In football, tackling and blocking – not in high faluting schemes. He believed you win on fundamentals. Whether dribbling a basketball, fielding a baseball or serving in tennis, your body has to be in the right position."

In the body politic, Robert E. Lee was always in position.

Chapter 2

Bob at Age 7

TOPEKA – WASHBURN – AND ROBERT E. LEE

Kansas, which became the nation's 34th state in 1861, adopted the slogan "Midway U.S.A." because it is the geographical center of the 48 coterminous United States.

In politics, "liberals," defined in the dictionary as those favorable to progress or reform, generally are deemed to be left of center. "Conservatives," those who agree with gradual rather than abrupt change and generally disposed to preserving existing conditions and institutions, are right of center.

There was never a doubt that Robert E. Lee, born March 15, 1914 in Topeka, Kansas, grew up to be right of center – a vowed conservative with a deep seated suspicion of big government.

His definition of liberal and conservative would have been much simpler and more direct: Liberal – tax and spend, big government; Conservative – less taxes, less government.

Bob was the second of three children parented by Meriam Florence (Maybelle) and Radcliffe Moore Lee. His older sister, Mildred Bernice, was born May 22, 1910, and Martha Jean, the youngest, arrived on November 12, 1919. Both were born in Topeka. All three were second generation Kansans.

Radcliffe

Mildred

Meriam

Bob and Mildred   **Bob and Martha**

Bob's father, Radcliffe, was born in 1881 on the Lee farm in Vernon Township, Cowley County, Kansas, and was baptized in the United Brethren Church in 1882. His mother, Meriam (Maybelle) was born in 1889 at Hymer, Kansas. Radcliffe and Meriam were married August 13, 1908 in Topeka.

Bob's grandfather Lee, the Reverend Phinneas Boothe Lee, was born in 1844 in Buchrus, Ohio. He married Bob's grandmother Lee, Laura Ellen Moore, in 1872 in Westerville, Ohio. They moved to

Bob, age 4 in front of family home in Topeka

Kansas in 1893 and settled on what became known as the Lee farm. On his maternal side, Bob's grandfather, Frank Napoleon Maybelle was born in Syracuse, New York in 1854 and came to Chase County, Kansas, (Hymer) when he was 20 years old. He met and married Bob's maternal grandmother, Sarah Lorraine Myers, in 1874, shortly after arriving in Kansas.

In 1898 the Lee family moved to Topeka where Reverend Phinneas Lee served for 11 years as Pastor of the Seabrook Congregational Church. The family had a modest home at 1020 West Street in Topeka, just across the street from a small municipal park. The Lee home is no longer there and the Topeka Public Library now occupies what was the small park that played such an important part of Bob's early life, since it contained two tennis courts.

Bob's Dad, Rad Lee, an outstanding athlete who was a star half-back at Washburn College in 1902–03, believed that Bob's physical stature, rather small and wiry, would limit his athletic endeavors to something less strenuous than football. (He was wrong. Bob, in his high school and college years ahead, would star in basketball and football as well as tennis.) Rad started teaching Bob tennis when he was six years old. Bob became very proficient at tennis, a game he loved all his life, and developed into a tournament caliber player in high school and college.

A WINNER – EVEN WITH WORDS

While Bob Lee was a tremendous high school athlete, starring in football, basketball and tennis, he also evinced a strong interest in democracy and government.

While in high school he won first place in state essay contests on the subjects of American history and the Constitution.

At Topeka High School, Bob not only was a good athlete and scholar but also a student leader. He was elected president of the Junior class in 1930. The high school annual, the Sunflower, had this to say about Bob: "When Coach Weaver was looking for a man to fill the veteran Kell's shoes, he tried out several men, but none quite measured up. Then Bob Lee stepped to the front, took charge of the

How Dad
looked when
he played
Half-Back
for Washbu
1902-03-
Weight 145

Dad at 21 years.

This is "Me"
and how I loo
when I play
quarter-ba
for Washbu
1933-'34-
and 1936-
I weighed 135
and 143-

I was 21 years.

Dad and Bob

13

Lee	Boyd	Swan	Seeman
President	Vice President	Secretary-Treasurer	Ch. Social Committee

Junior Class Officers

Tennis Squad
Bob – Top row on right

14

team and for the remainder of the season, ran it like a veteran. His headwork and strategy on the field were exceptionally good."

One of Bob's early role models was his high school football and basketball coach, an individual Bob continued to like and respect even after the coach threw him off the state high school championship basketball team for disciplinary reasons.

WHERE THERE'S SMOKE, THERE'S FIRING

Smoking was a life long habit of Bob Lee – one that he was unable to abandon even though it cost him his position on the state basketball championship team in high school.

Bob relates the story: "I was discovered smoking in the parking lot of the high school with two other players. Coach Weaver suspended us. He allowed the other two players to rejoin the team but I was out for the season because the coach said I was the leader and the other two were influenced by my bad example."

Bob who had to pay his own way in to watch his team play in the state finals, later commented: "This is where I first really found out that rules are rules – and if you violate them you pay the price."

The Sunflower Year Book described this coach, E. B. Weaver this way: "Tutoring our championship teams is as natural for Coach Weaver as eating. He possesses a rare faculty which enables him not only to instruct the athletes skillfully but also to instill into them the high qualities of sportsmanship for which every school strives. His football teams have lost one game in three seasons play, and the basketball team of 1932 won a state championship title."

Bob ended his high school career by earning, as a senior, the honor "T" for "excellence in activities, attendance, scholarship and contest."

While undoubtedly being influenced by his father, who was a graduate of Washburn College of Topeka, enrolling at Washburn was an easy choice for Bob because he was awarded a full athletic scholarship. Without the scholarship, it would have been difficult, if not impossible, for him to attend college, since the country was in the midst of the Great Depression. (The school was originally known as Lincoln College since tradition has it that President Lincoln gave a $25 gift towards its construction. The name was changed to Washburn College in 1868 when Ichabod Washburn gave a $25,000 gift. That also explains why the athletic teams are known as the Ichabods. In April, 1941, the citizens of Topeka voted to make the school a municipal university.)

Despite having the full scholarship and living at home during his first year at Washburn, Bob, a true "child of the Depression" always sought employment to help himself and his family during those precarious economic years. Throughout his college career, he worked at Menninger's Clinic, internationally known for its treatment of the mentally ill and those with alcoholic disorders, as the part time recreation director.

What was his best sport in college? It's hard to say. He earned nine letters, three each in football, basketball and tennis. Like most football players of his era, Bob played on both offense and defense. In addition, he was the punter and extra point man, specializing in that ancient and forgotten art – drop kicking. He did all this while weighing in at a hefty 135 pounds.

The Washburn football coach (for seven years, including the years Bob played) was Ernest Bearg. Bearg coached at Washburn for two years following his 1916 graduation but left Washburn to join the University of Illinois coaching staff. He then became head football coach at Nebraska where the Cornhuskers won 23, lost 7, and tied 3, winning their first of what was then known as the Big Six championship in 1928 with a 7–1–1 record. After that successful year, he returned to Washburn because the President of the College offered him a substantial raise to return and head up the physical education program as well as coach football.

He was once asked about what particular game in his long and illustrious coaching career was most memorable. "The Army game in 1934," he responded. "We lost 19–0, but Army scored all of its points in the final period. We had a 135 pound quarterback, Bobby Lee. You could tell the Cadets figured he had no business on the field with them, but after 60 minutes of punishing tackles (as well as playing defense), the Army players came to our dressing room and congratulated Lee for his courage and stamina."

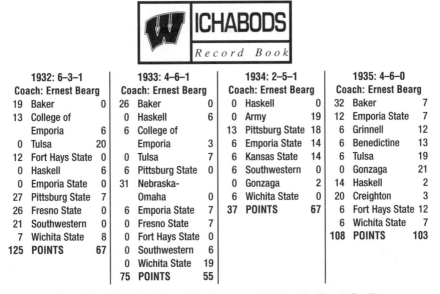

1932: 6–3–1		1933: 4–6–1		1934: 2–5–1		1935: 4–6–0	
Coach: Ernest Bearg		Coach: Ernest Bearg		Coach: Ernest Bearg		Coach: Ernest Bearg	
19 Baker	0	26 Baker	0	0 Haskell	0	32 Baker	7
13 College of		0 Haskell	6	0 Army	19	12 Emporia State	7
Emporia	6	6 College of		13 Pittsburg State	18	6 Grinnell	12
0 Tulsa	20	Emporia	3	6 Emporia State	14	6 Benedictine	13
12 Fort Hays State	0	0 Tulsa	7	6 Kansas State	14	6 Tulsa	19
0 Haskell	6	6 Pittsburg State	0	6 Southwestern	0	0 Gonzaga	21
0 Emporia State	0	31 Nebraska-		0 Gonzaga	2	14 Haskell	2
27 Pittsburg State	7	Omaha	0	6 Wichita State	0	20 Creighton	3
26 Fresno State	0	6 Emporia State	7	37 POINTS	67	6 Fort Hays State	12
21 Southwestern	0	0 Fresno State	7			6 Wichita State	7
7 Wichita State	8	0 Fort Hays State	0			108 POINTS	103
125 POINTS	67	0 Southwestern	6				
		0 Wichita State	19				
		75 POINTS	55				

**From the Ichabod's Record Book, as provided by Mr. Chuck Cordt,
Washburn University and Alumni Association Executive Director.**

Gonzaga had beaten Washington State that year and were unde-feated. Little Washburn played them in Spokane and held them scoreless until, as Bob put it: "I scored the only points in the game and we lost. I got a high pass from our center and it went into the end zone. I tried to run it out but never saw so many red jerseys in my life. The final score was 2–0."

Basketball followed football. Bob was a forward on the high school team and continued to play that position in college – and later in AAU (American Amateur Union) games.

In personal notes about his college athletic days, Bob said he "enjoyed playing because of the high competition we met." The Washburn Ichabods were in the Missouri Valley Conference which included such schools as Creighton, Drake, Grinnell, St. Louis University, Tulsa and the Oklahoma Aggies (later Oklahoma State.) The schedule had Washburn playing each of these teams twice with additional games against colleges such as DePaul, Wisconsin, Kansas State and Kansas.

All-Time Washburn Scores

1932–33: 8–6 Coach: George Gardner			1933–34: 7–8 Coach: Elmer Holm			1934–35: 7–13 Coach: Elmer Holm			1935–36: 7–14 Coach: Elmer Holm		
39	Haskell	28	31	Ottawa	23	17	Pittsburg State	30	38	Kansas State	58
29	Bethany	17	25	Phillips	29	22	Wichita State	33	18	Kansas	35
28	Phillips	38	37	Ottawa	27	19	Southwestern	39	28	Kansas State	29
39	Wichita State	61	33	Southwestern	35	21	Baker	34	38	St. Louis	25
35	Emporia State	31	57	Haskell	25	27	Washington	28	25	DePaul	43
35	College of Emporia	33	31	Emporia State	33	28	Drake	41	27	Wisconsin	36
29	Baker	13	20	Pittsburg State	23	19	Grinnell	28	28	Grinnell	29
38	Fort Hays State	40	33	Emporia State	37	31	Tulsa	28	29	Washington	36
36	Pittsburg State	34	19	Fort Hays State	40	32	Wichita State	31	29	Wichita State	34
32	Southwestern	23	23	Southwestern	27	26	Oklahoma State	27	24	Tulsa	26
23	Wichita State	51	27	Pittsburg State	22	26	Oklahoma State	25	21	Oklahoma State	43
40	Emporia State	50	28	Nebraska-Omaha	26	32	Grinnell	51	27	Oklahoma State	29
39	College of Emporia	34	43	College of Emporia	33	27	Kansas	33	42	Grinnell	41
36	Pittsburg State	43	27	College of Emporia	23	25	Baker	32	37	Drake	26
478	**POINTS**	**496**	22	Kansas	31	28	Creighton	32	42	Washington	30
			572	**POINTS**	**650**	35	Pittsburg	19	39	Creighton	35
						45	Washington	30	34	Tulsa	24
						41	Drake	57	32	Wichita State	44
						33	Creighton	32	36	Drake	38
						38	Tulsa	20	33	Creighton	32
						572	**POINTS**	**650**	30	Kansas	33
									657	**POINTS**	**726**

Probably "the big game" of Bob's college basketball career was in 1936 when Washburn was competing for the right to represent the Midwest District in the Olympic trials.

Oklahoma A. & M., coached by the incomparable Henry Iba, had defeated Nebraska, 36 to 19, in the first semi-final game in Kansas City. The next semi-final was the University of Kansas coached by the equally famous Dr. Phog Allen against Washburn.

Following is a newspaper story about that game: "Pralle, the Kansas guard went sprawling under the clever little Lee, Washburn forward. Rising, Pralle, delivered a vigorous kick at his opponent and was promptly called for fouling. The crowd chose this incident to vent its wrath on the Jayhawkers. Until the finish the Ichabods had the arena tormenters on their side.

18

**Bob Lee,
basketball forward**

"At the end of the first half the score was tied at 14 each, but starting the second half, the Big Six conference champions forgot personalities and indulged in basketball to such an extent, they quickly had a commanding lead. With about 5 minutes to play, the University led 30 to 20. Then began an exhibition of shooting the likes of which has been rarely seen.

"Washburn pulled to within 31 to 30, but Kansas made the final basket and won 33 to 30. Washburn had its stars. Lee, a little forward, twice drove in for goals against Collard, the center, and Fee (Joe Fee, the other forward on Bob's high school team) began his pyrotechnics – three baskets in a row. They were thrilling while they lasted."

As good as he was in both these sports, tennis probably was his best sport.

**Washburn swept the Missouri Valley conference tournament
at Tulsa, Oklahoma (Bob Lee on far left)**

In addition to working at the Menninger Clinic, Bob conducted a tennis class in the summer while at Washburn. He continued to play tennis most of his life and during his early Denver years competed in both singles and doubles play.

His son, Eric, recalls that his father was vicious on the tennis court.

19

"No matter who was on the other side of the net," Eric recalled, "Dad would show no mercy. Didn't matter whether it was a tournament or a friendly game with family, even Mom. When a deciding point was at issue, he would go for the jugular."

He was a marvelous coach but also a task master. "Dad was very, very competitive," Eric said, "and he expected perfection from those he taught. I recall when Mom wanted to learn to play tennis, Dad said, 'until you know how to hit the ball, you're not playing in any match with anybody.'"

And he was very deceptive. "Players thought he didn't have a strong serve or couldn't run, or had no backhand," Eric said, "but he showed them up completely by running them all over the court while he didn't even work up a sweat."

For two years he was captain of the tennis team that won the Missouri Valley Conference title and with a teammate, Carl Nordstrom, won the doubles championship.

Alpha Delta House

He was elected President of the Alpha Delts his senior year (one of his fraternity members was Ward Bushacher who moved to Denver and became Mayor Dick Batterton's Manager of Revenue in 1959, after Bob took on the responsibility for getting Batterton elected.) From that position Bob campaigned and was elected Student Council President. When Bob attended Washburn there were four fraternities and sororities. The fraternities were Alpha

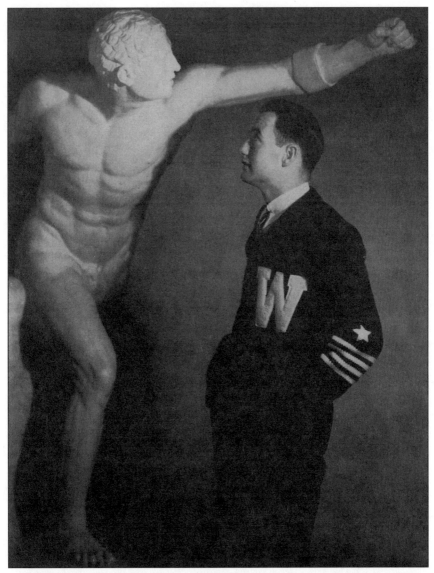

Master craftsman on the athletic field is Bob Lee. It takes cunning to guide the modern football machine – Lee did it three years. It takes quick-thinking to function as "spark-plug" on a present-day basketball quintet – Lee earned two letters on the hardwood court. It requires intricate knowledge to master tennis problems – Lee captained the team this year, led it to the Missouri Valley championship. (From KAW, the Washburn College yearbook)

Delta, Phi Alpha Delta, Phi Delta Theta and Kappa Sigma. The sororities were Alpha Phi, Delta Gamma, Kappa Alpha Theta and Zeta Tau Alpha. When elections for Class Officer came around there were two political parties and each party consisted of two fraternities and two sororities. Since the Independents constituted the vast majority of the students, the winning party was always the one that got the majority of the Independent votes. Even at Washburn Bob was considered to be an expert in such campaigns. This activity certainly stimulated his interest in politics.

In his senior year at Washburn, he was honored by being named Letterman of the Year. There was a full page in his senior yearbook devoted to his athletic accomplishments and records he set. He was initiated into the Sagamore Society, the senior men's honor society. He was selected for displaying "salient scholarship, leadership and character and has shown unselfish service to the college." It was the highest honor a student could receive at Washburn.

Not all of Bob's time was spent playing various sports, studying and working. He found time to date several girls at Topeka and Washburn. One of them, Betty Fallin, relates that her best friend was Peggy Ann Landon, daughter of Alf Landon's first wife. The two girls were in Bob's high school class at Topeka High and the boys and girls who were Peggy's friends would gather at the Governor's Mansion at 8th and Buchanan every Friday night. They would babysit Peggy Ann Landon's baby sister Nancy, who was born of Alf's second wife and who later became U.S. Senator Nancy Kassabaum.

Bob did not graduate from college. After his fourth year he and a football team friend left Kansas for California and summer work. They went to Sacramento, California where Bob worked for a Coca Cola distributing firm during the day and played AAU basketball for the Spalding Sports Company in the evenings.

The "summer sabbatical" lasted two years when Bob returned to Topeka with the intention of reentering Washburn and studying law.

President, Student Council

WASHBURN
REVISITED

It was a typical fall, pre-registration day at Washburn College in Topeka. Elizabeth Johnston, who had decided to transfer to Washburn after completing her freshman year at Lindenwood College in St. Charles, Missouri and a girl friend, Rosemary Young

Part of Washburn Campus, including football field, basketball arena, and Alpha Delta House

Littlefield were strolling along a campus street, chatting about courses and classes.

"Two boys in a nice convertible drove by, honked the horn and whistled," Elizabeth remembers. "They went around the block, came back, and whistled again. We stopped at a nearby inn for a coke and there they were." One of the boys was Robert E. Lee, who had returned to the Washburn campus after a two year sojourn in California.

"They knew Rosemary and Bob asked her to introduce him to me," Elizabeth said. "We had a nice chat and I went back to the dorm expecting him to call. But he did not call that night."

Bob had intended to call Elizabeth, a native of Colorado, and a graduate of South High School in Denver, but had gotten the telephone number of a different Elizabeth.

"He finally got the right number and we started dating," Elizabeth recalls. "But remember, we were in the middle of a Depression and Bob was very poor, so he really wouldn't ask me for dates but would just happen to meet me at school dances. On Sundays he would pick me up and we would go out for a picnic, with Bob's mother supplying the picnic lunch. I continued to date Bobby during the remainder of 1938 and the spring of 1939, even though someone in my sorority told me that Bob Lee was the type who would 'love me and leave me.'"

GENERALLY SPEAKING. . .

Robert E. (for Erwin) Lee was not related to General Robert E. (Edward) Lee, but the name similarity gained him unwanted publicity while he was a student at Washburn. The following story appeared in the Topeka newspaper: "Seventy years ago today, Robert E. Lee, a Confederate General, was lodged in Richmond, Virginia, with not a thought of surrendering the city. Today, Robert E. Lee, a 19-year old student living at 2408 Hantoon Street, was driving along with no thought of surrender. A gendarme, however, claimed he was driving too fast, so Robert Lee – not General – was arrested."

Clipped to that story, in Bob's personal files, was a receipt from the City of Topeka Police Department, with the case number duly noted, for payment of a $10 fine.

Much more devastating to Elizabeth (better known as Bee), however, was being informed by her parents that the Dean of Women, Susan Guild, at Washburn had written to them and told them that "in my opinion Elizabeth should not date Robert E. Lee. He is not good for her."

Susan Guild

They were married on June 3, 1939, in Independence, Missouri. The marriage ended 59 years later, at Bob's death. "Now that I think about it," Bee reminisced, "Bobby really never proposed. As the end of the school year approached in May, he just told me 'we're going to get married.'"

Their best friends, Jiggs and Peggy Shaefor, drove with them to Independence. They found a Justice of the Peace working in a shoe store and he agreed to perform the ceremony.

Returning to Topeka after a very short honeymoon, "one or two days," Bee said, "Bob found himself without employment. He had rejoined Menninger Clinic as the Recreation Director, but the job was abolished because of Depression caused cutbacks."

Since Bee's parents were unaware of the marriage, the young couple decided Bee should return to Denver, stay with her parents, tell them the "big news" while Bob stayed in Topeka to find work.

"I told my parents about being married the morning after I arrived home," Bee said. "Their reaction was immediate and firm. They told me to pack up, they were taking me back to Topeka, that since I was married my place was with Bob."

Bob's mother did not take the news as well. She wanted the marriage annulled. In fact, when Bee and her parents arrived at Bob's parents' house, Mrs. Lee refused to come down from her bedroom to meet her new in-laws. "Mr. Lee finally persuaded her to come down and meet my parents," Bee said, "but she certainly wasn't very gracious."

After this meeting in the Lee home, the Johnstons returned to Denver with Bee and her newly acquired husband in tow. One of Bee's relatives had a cabin in Turkey Creek and she and Bob had a belated honeymoon there.

"Even though my mother was not one to make friends easily," Bee said, "she really came to like Bobby through the years. He talked politics with her by the hour and she loved every minute of it. That's just the way Bobby was with women."

Bee's parents bought them a new car as a wedding present and they returned to Topeka. There, Bob and a friend, Bill Edmonston, worked out an agreement to lease a gasoline station. Since money was scarce they agreed that Bill would live with them. They had found an upstairs apartment in a home nearby.

A PLANNED EVICTION

Bob had not yet entered the real estate profession when he and Bee rented their first apartment in Topeka but he was able to terminate a lease - and get a full month's rent returned. Bee recalls they discovered the apartment on the second floor of the house did not have a sink and they had to wash dishes in the bath tub. They discovered a loose board in the floor directly over the landlady's bedroom. They took turns rocking the board all night. "The next morning she asked us to move and refunded our money," Bee said. "I guess she knew we were newlyweds and her imagination did the rest."

Later, they located an apartment closer to the filling station and lived there for almost a year. "This place had a yard, so I bought a dog for Bob and two kittens for myself," Bee remembers. "Bill stayed with us and happily offered to babysit the pets whenever Bob and I wanted to go out."

They barely eked out a living operating the filling station and so decided to sell it and "leave Topeka to seek our fortune," Bee said. She recalls that they had won a raffle of some kind, so "we had $25 and a radio when we left Topeka," and drove to Galveston, Texas, where they arrived on June 3, the first anniversary of their marriage and spent the day "getting sunburned on the beach." Then they travelled on to Lubbock where Bob knew someone who had worked

26

with him at Menninger's but the friend was unable to help Bob get employment.

"By this time we were down to our last 25 cents," Bee said. "We didn't like the idea, but we had no alternative but to wire my folks and ask for some money."

Bee's father agreed to send the money on condition that "you use it to drive to Denver." They did and moved in with Bee's parents in their home at 452 South Ogden Street. Bee's father, Earl Johnston, had a real estate business at 280 South Downing. Bob started learning the business from his father-in-law but Denver was not yet in its real estate boom days, so Bob took a job as a sales person with Cottrell's Men's Store in Downtown Denver.

This was a tumultuous time, not only in Bob's and Bee's lives but also for the entire nation. Europe was already involved in World War II, the United States was assisting the allies with supplies of food, machinery, equipment, ships and planes and generally gearing up for war-time production. Bob was studying for his real estate broker's license while working at Cottrell's and also playing AAU basketball. Then there were numerous tennis matches - and Bee was pregnant with Eric. He was born on February 17, 1941.

Always on the alert for a better job and additional income, Bob learned about a major construction company, The Peter Kiewit Co., that had just won a major army contract to build additional barracks at Fort Carson. Bob sold himself directly to Peter Kiewit, whose company headquarters were in Omaha, Nebraska, and was hired as an assistant personnel manager. This position necessitated a move to Grand Island, Nebraska, where Kiewit had established a branch office to recruit personnel to replace the men who were going into the service.

Bob was convinced women could be as effective as men in these jobs and launched a four-state area recruiting program to bring females into the construction trades. The recruiting program, as outlined in the Kiewit company records, featured "Rosie the Riveter," "Cathy the Carpenter," and "Tammy the Truckdriver."

After the United States entered World War II on December 7, 1941, Bob was uncomfortable staying out of the service even though he had a defense industry deferment and was married and had one child. He tried to enlist but when the recruiter found out his age, almost 27, his marital status and the job he was holding, he was rejected. So they bought a house in Grand Island and Bob continued to work for the Kiewit company, recruiting and training personnel, mostly female, for the rapidly expanding company.

"Bob made a bargain with me," Bee remembers. "He said he would wait until his 30th birthday and then would try to enlist again after returning to Denver which we planned to do." That move was hastened when Bee became pregnant. She returned to Denver where their second child, Denny, was born on July 30, 1943.

As the war escalated, military man power demands increased and Bob was able to enlist as a Corpsman in the Navy. After Boot Camp he was sent to Guam where he was stationed at a military hospital.

Bob in the Navy

"The Navy knew of his athletic background so gave him additional recreation duties," Bee remembers. "There were many well known athletes there, including such major league baseball players as Peewee Reese of the Brooklyn Dodgers, who became a close friend of Bob's." Many games were played in the evening and Bob, who was not a baseball player, manned the microphone and gave play-by- play description of the games.

Bob was discharged from the Navy in 1945 and returned home on Christmas Eve of that year. "During the holidays, Bob made contact with Mr. Kiewit who asked him to come to Omaha to meet with him and talk about his future," Bee recalls. "Bob did go to Omaha, met with Mr. Kiewit who offered him a position. Bob stayed overnight in Omaha. Then, after thinking over the proposition, told Mr. Kiewit that he had been away from his family too long and wanted to make his home in Denver."

Bob returned to Denver where the family continued to live with Bee's parents and Bob again joined Earl Johnston in his real estate

Eric, Bee, Denny, Bob

business. Later Bob and Bee moved into their own home at 152 South Downing Street, just one block away from the office.

Bob satisfied his appetite for athletic competition by playing AAU basketball with Bob McCurdy, Roscoe Walker, Vince Boryla, Lefty Martin and others as well as becoming a coach of football and baseball teams in the Young America League in Denver.

"Eric was old enough to start getting involved and even though it meant many late dinners, I was happy to see them together," Bee said. "And Bob really enjoyed working with those youngsters."

In 1950, the Lee family purchased a building site at 1040 South Gilpin and constructed a home there. The back yard of the house featured a half court, almost regulation size, basketball court. It was here that Bob taught Eric and Denny the basketball skills that enabled them to become star high school and college basketball players.

"We spent many a day and night on that half court and could play at night because Dad had installed floodlights," Eric relates. "We would come out after dinner and practice free throws, the first to lose would have to go in and do the dishes." The Lee basketball court and Bob's coaching was available to all the neighborhood kids. "We had wonderful times there," Eric said, "and some really good competitive basketball games."

Bob had time for other activities as well, such as visiting with neighbors. It was one of the neighborly visits with Mae Willis that launched Bob into organizational politics, a life long passion.

AAU Team

Chapter 4

**Bob & Jim Johnson from
Young America League**

POLITICAL
BAPTISM

Mae Willis, a friendly neighbor listened as Bob Lee expressed his concerns about big government. She nodded approvingly. Bob indicated he feared President Roosevelt's New Deal programs being carried out and expanded by President Truman, were putting the country on the road to socialism. Mae Willis' eyes sparkled. Furthermore, the country needed a conservative president like Alf Landon of Kansas or Robert Taft of Ohio. Mae Willis smiled - she knew she had a new recruit. Mae was a long time worker in the political party and was Vice Chairman of the Denver Republican Party at the time Bob Lee was engaging her in political chit chat.

Soon she was talking to him about party politics, the precinct caucus which elected delegates to the County Assembly where it was decided who would go to the State Convention where decisions were made as to who would be on the ballot as official party candidates for public office. And this process would determine who would go to the party's National Convention and participate in selecting the candidate to run for the presidency of the United

States. Bob was intrigued and converted. Working through an organization like this, mobilizing and utilizing the skills of others to elect candidates to offices, was, in Bob's mind, a better way to accomplish his conservative goals than running for office.

He knew how to run for office. He had been elected president of his junior class at Topeka High School. He ran for and was elected president of the student council at Washburn College. He had also organized political campaigns for others during his college days.

Since 1952 was a presidential year and President Truman had announced that he would not be running for another term, Bob decided it was a good time to become involved in the Republican Party organization. He accepted Mae's offer to become a committeeman in his precinct. Bob had a knack for talking with people, particularly on the telephone, and drawing them out about their concerns and their desires and, particularly, what they would like to do for the Republican Party. Once someone expressed an interest, he gave them a job to do. No matter how trivial or how important the job might be, Bob made it clear that he expected regular progress reports until the task was accomplished.

Before accepting the appointment from Mae Willis, Bob had already determined whom he would support for the presidency - U. S. Senator Robert Taft of Ohio. He was convinced Taft, because of his conservative record and his many years of experience as a Republican Senator, would have little difficulty in defeating another potential candidate, World War II General and hero Dwight Eisenhower. He also learned that another conservative Senator that he admired, Eugene Milliken of Colorado, was closely allied with Senator Taft.

Knowing how the system worked, Bob got himself elected to the Denver County Assembly as a Taft delegate and to the State Convention, again as a Taft delegate. Because of Senator Milliken's political stature and influence, the national GOP was confident Colorado's 17 delegates would go to Taft and very little internal campaigning was accomplished in the state. That was Bob's first lesson in internal Colorado Republican politics: Never assume your choice is a lock; never assume that simply because your precinct is safe for your candidate that all others are; and do not overestimate the influence of one individual. While Bob was disappointed that Taft was not selected, he was pleased that Eisenhower was elected President of the United States, particularly since he had selected Richard Nixon, a young conservative Congressman from California, as his Vice President.

Family picture, Denny, Eric, Delisa, Bob, Bee

Politically, the last half of 1952 and 1953 were quiet years but family and business responsibilities increased. Bob and Bee's third child, Delisa, was born June 9, 1952.

He was coaching the Redskins, a Young America League football team, and son, Eric, now 11, and Denny, now 9, were playing football in this league. In addition, he was coaching them and others regularly in basketball, playing tennis and teaching Bee and others how to play that game.

JUNIOR 'B'

FRONT ROW:
    JIM JELTEMA, CORKY DOUGLASS, DALE DETER, BILLY MOODY, LARRY AIKEN, WALLY BECKETT
MIDDLE ROW:
    BOBBY JOHNSON, DAVEY JONES, HUGH MacMILLEN, STARR VELLAND, PETE VERGA,   SHAW,

BACK ROW:
    BOB LEE, JIM JOHNSON, KENT ANDERSON, LANCE SLOCUM, STEVE THOMPSON, STEVE JACKSON, JOHN SPYKSTRA,
                                                                        VI JONES, MGR.

SEASON
LEAGUE RECORD —
            7 WON   — 0 LOST

SOUTH DIVISION PLAYOFF:
            REDSKINS 33 —— WILDCATS 0

CITY CHAMPIONSHIP
            REDSKINS 2 — ROUGH RIDERS 6

Redskins – names and season record

34

He decided to venture out on his own in the real estate business and formed a partnership with a life long friend, Jim Aspinwall.

LOCATION, LOCATION, LOCATION - AND CONTACTS

Because he spent so much time as a non-paid party worker, Bob's work in real estate sometimes suffered. Nonetheless, he was successful and got his broker's license. His wife, Bee, explains his success this way: "Little old ladies particularly loved him. I guess he looked like he needed mothering. In any event, they would find properties and intercede on his behalf for the listing."

Learning basketball fundamentals under their father's tutelage at 1040 South Gilpin on the "family half court," paid off for both Eric and Denny. They starred in basketball at South High and were awarded basketball scholarships at the University of Colorado.

He did not ignore politics, however. As precinct committeeman he was getting acquainted with Republicans in his area and becoming acquainted with individuals who would be life long friends - Ralph Clark, Paul Hodges, Jim Aspinwall, Ed Alexander, Rendle Myer, Don Blanchard and other post-World War II "young Republicans" who began changing the Denver GOP structure and replacing the old guard with new and younger faces.

In 1954, the Democratic Party was dominant. Ed Johnson was Governor, Byron Rogers perennially was Denver's United States Congressman, and John Carroll, former Democratic District Attorney and House member, was elected to the U. S. Senate. The Democrats controlled both Houses of the State Legislature.

In Denver, Mayor Quigg Newton was leaving that office but popular Democratic District Attorney, Bert Keating, of Denver, was looking toward running for that office in 1955. So was Ernest Maranzino, a veteran eight year City Councilman from North Denver.

Republicans needed a candidate to run for Mayor. They found him in Will Nicholson, a graduate of Dartmouth College, well respected in Denver business circles, a Reserve Air Force Brigadier General, and a two-term Colorado State Senator. He had also been active in President Eisenhower's campaign and was known nationally.

The 1955 Denver mayoralty race was unique in that it was necessary, because of a Charter change, for a candidate to have 50% of the votes cast. Prior to that, if there were several candidates, the candidate with the most votes would win, even though the vote total might be less than 50% of the votes cast.

In the first election, Keating commanded 53,339 votes, Nicholson 51,699 and Marranzino 5,626. But because Keating's total was only 45% of the total votes cast, there had to be a runoff election. Keating was heavily favored but Nicholson won.

Ralph Clark, Nicholson's organization leader recounts the excitement of that race and Nicholson's come from behind victory.

"I had assigned three Southeast districts containing 62 precincts to Bob Lee to work as an area leader for Nicholson," Clark said. "Bob recruited over a dozen Republican precinct leaders where there were none, encouraged all of them to recruit block workers and to turn out the vote for Nicholson. He had each of his precinct leaders make their official counts and take the extra time to recount the large number of votes and make sure of the tallies before delivering the official results to the Election Commission.

"It was 20 of these 62 precincts that tipped the scale for Nicholson, who won by 766 votes. Even after Keating demanded a recount, Nicholson still won and increased his margin to 820 votes."

This election proved to Clark, Lee and other young Republicans that they now had an organization in Denver that could compete and beat the Democrats.

For his part in the campaign, Bob received one of the few rewards he ever accepted for his political activities – appointment by Mayor Nicholson, to be Clerk and Recorder for the City and County of Denver. It wasn't much of a reward because the job paid only $6,000 a year. (The mayor's salary then was set in the Charter at $14,000 annually.) In addition, the job carried the responsibility of chairing the Denver Election Commission. He succeeded Paul Hodges, Jr., who then was appointed a municipal judge by Nicholson.

(Lee resigned the City Clerk position after being elected Denver Republican Party Chairman in March of 1958. Lee's successor as

Clerk and Recorder, was Charles Byrne, who, in later years, was elected Auditor of Denver and was unsuccessful in a bid to become Mayor of Denver in 1975.)

In early 1956, the young Republicans who cut their political teeth in the Nicholson election, decided it was time to have a showdown meeting with party leaders. This group included, among others, Bob Lee, Ralph Clark, Bill Powers, Jim Aspinwall, Ed Alexander, Rendle Myer and Don Blanchard. They met with Charlie Armstrong, County Chairman; Mae Willis, Vice Chairman; and Tom McCarthy, Secretary, and talked about what they perceived as a need for new and more aggressive leadership.

The meeting resulted in a compromise. Charlie, Mae and Tom would stay in office until 1958 when Bob, Ralph and Rendle would officially run for the offices with the incumbent officers' enthusiastic support. This agreement gave the new leaders time to recruit party workers to fill vacancies in districts and precincts throughout the city. Rather than ousting long time captains and causing hard feelings that would hurt the party, the new leaders decided to leave them in office but place their own key people in strategic positions as area leaders to coordinate activities in several districts.

In 1958, by unanimous vote, Bob Lee was elected Chairman of the Denver Republican Party; Georgia Middlemist, Vice Chairman; Ralph Clark, Secretary; and Rendle Myer, Treasurer. By this time they had assembled a list of workers, many of whom had been active in Eisenhower's reelection campaign in 1956, and leadership positions were filled. That list, in Bob's handwriting, is on page 38.

Brimming with confidence, the Denver Republican political organization looked forward to turning out the Republican vote in the 1958 election for governor and defeating the popular incumbent, Steven L. R. McNichols.

The Republicans nominated Palmer L. Burch, a veteran House member who chaired the powerful Joint Budget Committee. Frank L. Hays, another popular legislator from Denver, ran for the position of Lieutenant Governor as a Republican while Robert L. Knous, son of former Colorado Governor, Lee Knous, was the Democratic choice for Lieutenant Governor. Bob introduced into the campaign an issue that he espoused throughout his political life - the "right to

	Captains		[illegible] Men
	Jack Schmidt	Christine Bouton	Pittroff
	Marian Haigs	Frances Webster	Hodges
	Jay Black	Mary Lou Fringe	Shoemaker
	Bill Samuelson	Terry Jones	Rolander
—	Frank Southworth	Roseanne Ball	Aspinwall
—	Bob Renshaw	Jean Williams	Alexander
—	Jim Freese	Annette Hollingsworth	Ned Heffenstiel
—	Bart Falasco	Betty Unfug	Ruskin
	Jim Johnson	Helen Johnson	Randle Meyer
X	Gene Howell	Barbara Anderson	Charles Byrne
	Bill Webster	Jean Meyer	Chas Lindsey
—	Larry Perry	Esther Aspegren	~~[illegible]~~
	Don Dominick	Pearl Ewatt	Len Pyatt
	~~William Karcher~~	~~Ruth Clark~~	~~Tom Fick~~
	Sidney Goldman	Carol Pyatt	Carl Schmid
—	Lou Middleswood	Bobby MacDougal	Walt Kristich
	Neil Jones	Vera Underhill	Ed Baker
X	Bob Sims	Vera Schneider	Jim Carder
	Carl Staker	Carol Cogley	Sterling Kahn
	Amos Lackey	Jean Wycoff	Lee Woods
ace Diner	Paul West	Mary Wycoff	Bud Horner
Bill Wagner	Bob Watkins	Betty Pifford	Al Schold
Henry Hennies	Jack Ehrhart	Peggy Griffin	Bruce Denig
Carl Dole—	Jim Eitemiller	Bessie Anderson	Ralph Clark
Bob Yeggy	John Duggan	Jane Gormsey	Dwight Hamilton
	Bob Arnold	Hilda Nichols	Jack Kellogg
	Chas Armstrong	Connie Cottrell	John Sommers
—	Fred Harding	Bobbe Tomey	
	Bud Stephens	Thelma Schmelzle	
	Joe Meyers	Connie Kruse	
	Ed Baker	Varetia Schaaf	
	[illegible] McBride		
	Joe P[illegible]d		

work concept." Existing state law made it possible for unions to negotiate "closed shop" contracts with employers, which meant that a worker, once hired, had to join that union and pay dues.

"It just flies in the face of the Declaration of Independence and our entire democratic process," Bob said on many occasions. The "right to work" issue obviously was vigorously opposed by organized labor.

Governor McNichols remained the people's choice as he decisively beat Burch in the general election on November 4, 1958. It was a disastrous beginning for Lee in his first year at the helm of the Denver Republican party.

Statewide, McNichols received 321,165 votes to 228,643 for Burch. In Denver County, McNichols won by even a larger percentage – 107,645 votes to 64,744 for Burch.

Knous was elected Lieutenant Governor, 299,835 to 236,577 for Hays. In Denver Knous garnered 98,819 votes to 68,051 for Hays. In 1958, before districting, all candidates for the House and Senate in Denver ran at large. Not one Republican of 17 candidates for the House and 8 in the Senate won.

Bob and his cohorts were disappointed but looked at the defeat as part of a learning process. They started regrouping to get ready for the Denver mayoralty election in 1959.

Mayor Nicholson decided not to seek reelection and the obvious Republican candidate was Richard Y. Batterton, owner of a car dealership in Denver and Manager of Public Works during the Nicholson administration.

**ELECTING A MAYOR
AND BUILDING AN
ORGANIZATION**

Tom Gavin's "Political Profile"

The City and County of Denver has a non-partisan form of government. Candidates for elective office gain a place on the ballot through the petition process and not through the convention nominating process of political parties.

"Nothing on the ballot shall be indicative of the source of the candidacy or of the support of any candidate. No ballot shall have printed thereon any party or political designation or mark, and there shall not be appended to the name of any candidate any party or political designation or mark, or anything indicating his views or opinions."
– Section C1.7-2 Denver City Charter

Richard Yates Batterton, who served as Manager of Public Works during the Nicholson administration, was a perfect "non-partisan" candidate. He was a business man and had not been involved in internal party politics. In his book, *The Old Gray Mayors of Denver*, the late George Kelly reviewed that election and noted that each candidate was asked why he was seeking the position.

Batterton responded: "It (public office) gets in your blood and you can't help wanting to continue what you started. Perhaps I ought to have my head examined for seeking such a job. I don't need the job. But I do have a genuine love for the city and feel that because of my experience in business and public life, I can make a contribution to good, clean, progressive government."

Organization workers were not handcuffed by the non-partisan language of the City Charter. Parties worked on behalf of candidates whose political affiliation was well known.

DEMOCRATS ARE OKAY – SOMETIMES

Bob Lee had no qualms about crossing political lines to help his candidate win an election. While managing Richard Batterton's campaign for Mayor of Denver, he met with Sam Lusky, at that point in time a liberal Democrat. "Are you a Democrat?" Lee asked Lusky. Sam answered in the affirmative. "Are you one of those P.R. guys (public relations) who are in it just for the money? How do I know you'll be committed?" Sam replied: "I hate to lose." Lee hired him on the spot.

Bob Lee, who was appointed Batterton's campaign director early on, said this to a colleague: "Dick is hung up on this non-partisan stuff. But he's a Republican and we're going to get him elected by going door to door in every precinct in Denver. I've got two captains in southeast Denver who need help, Vera Schneider and Leonard Davis. They're good Republicans but they don't have half of the committeemen and committeewomen spots filled in District 35. I want you to call on them and tell them I sent you to help them in every way and let them know you're not after their jobs because you don't even live in their district. Also tell them you will be helping the captains in District 34, Penny Griffin and Bob Arnold, as well as Bob Rosenheim and Betty Unfug, the captains in District 36." (This "directive" was given to the author of this book, Joe Shoemaker.)

The Democratic Party, meanwhile, was gnashing its teeth because Will Nicholson, a Republican, had become Mayor of what historically had been a "Democratic" city and now the Deputy Mayor, Dick Batterton, wanted to continue Republican control of that office.

The problem for the Democratic Party was that not one but two strong candidates declared for the office – Roland L. (Sonny)

Mapelli and George A. Cavender. Mapelli, a relative newcomer to politics who was just finishing his first term on the Denver City Council, had strong support from Denver's north side.

Cavender's great strength was his relationship with organized labor, where he had served as president of the Colorado Labor Council. In addition, Cavender was a member of City Council and its president at the time of his announcement. Lee viewed Mapelli as the stronger of the two Democratic candidates and his analysis was substantiated by a Denver Post poll conducted two weeks before the May 19th election that showed Mapelli favored by 25% of Denver voters, Batterton 21%, and Cavender 17%.

Lee latched on to the fact that former Councilman Ed Mapel, who had resigned from City Council to become vice president of the Sahara Hotel and Casino in Las Vegas, was an active supporter of Mapelli's. George Kelly reported in his book that "by linking Mapelli to Mapel, the Denver Post tried to show that Sonny might be beholden to Nevada gambling interests and thus, by association, susceptible to vague, wicked influences."

Lee called his key people together and underscored this point and told them to use this information with all their precinct and door-to-door workers. Lee's

Mayor Richard Batterton

43

strategy paid off. Denver voters on May 19 put Batterton ahead with 52,386 votes; Cavender second, 38,455; and Mapelli dropped to 33,869.

Batterton supporters were overjoyed but immediately recognized that those voters supporting Mapelli would make a difference in the June runoff election. Cavender supporters were also aware of this and so both candidates sought support from the Mapelli camp. Mapelli declined to openly endorse either.

George Kelly credits Bob Lee with making the difference in the runoff election. "Bob Lee, as he was to do later. . . in Claude M. Kirk, Jr.'s campaign in Florida, demonstrated Republican organizational ability that turned lackadaisical uncertainty into victory," Kelly said. "By carefully studying precincts where Batterton had made poor showings in the election and then buttressing the weak spots through cajoling and recruiting, Lee transformed the Denver GOP into a power with political muscle. Bob was hailed as a miracle worker, not only in Denver, but later, nationally." Batterton received 58,016, Cavender 50,305 in the runoff.

After the election Lee continued to counsel Batterton and recommended individuals for city positions. Among those appointed by Batterton were Robert Rolander, County Court Administrator; Paul Hodges, Manager of Welfare; Ward Bushacher, Manager of Revenue; and Joe Shoemaker, Administrative Assistant in the Office of the Mayor.

With the Republican organization in Denver in place and a track record of success in the Batterton election, Lee directed his attention to the presidential election, Vice President Nixon vs. Senator John Kennedy and the State Legislature, with the intention of gaining GOP control of both Houses. (The governor's term had been increased to four years from two in 1958.)

In 1958, his first year, as the head of the Denver Republican Party, the "right to work" issue did not catch on and Governor McNichols won that election by a landslide, defeating the Republican candidate Palmer L. Burch, a veteran Denver legislator. While that election was a disappointment, Bob later recalled an event that influenced his political and personal life thereafter – his first meeting with Richard Nixon.

"It was in the fall of 1958 prior to the election," notes from Bob's personal papers indicate. "I had just been elected the Republican County Chairman of Denver. The Democrats controlled both Houses of the Legislature, the Governor and Lieutenant Governor, all four of our Congressmen and one of the U.S. Senators.

"My first job was to try to pump some life back in the Party. I sent out a call for the Vice President. He immediately accepted and we had a rally at East High School in Denver. To show the lack of interest, the most we could turn out was about 800 loyal Republicans. Both the Vice President and Mrs. Nixon were very patient with our rather meager effort. At least it probably was a beginning. Although I had a very limited opportunity to visit, I was completely dedicated to the Vice President from that time on."

This same memorandum continued: "Again in 1959 the Vice President stopped over in Denver to speak to a small group of financially affluent Republicans in a fund raising effort. He (the Vice President) asked Eddie Nicholson (Vice President of Public Affair for United Air Lines and a prominent Republican in national circles) and me to meet him at the airport so we could talk a few minutes before his commercial plane departed.

"The three of us stood out there between a couple of parked cars and discussed the coming presidential election. By that time I could control Colorado's situation and told him that if he decided to run he could start with a guarantee of 18 delegate votes from Colorado and we could carry the state in the general election. I believed he accepted that at face value.

"Although the Colorado laws prohibited a legally bound and a committed delegation, those delegates were hand picked and at our State Convention we had a resolution introduced and passed that stated that Richard Nixon should be the one and only candidate. Our 18 delegates did cast their votes for Nixon and we carried the state in November by 90,000+ majority."

Races for state offices showed remarkable gains in 1960, even though Nixon nationally was defeated by Kennedy for President.

Lee was becoming well known in national Republican politics, in State Republican politics and Denver Republican politics. But his work was not generally recognized until Tom Gavin, the political reporter for the Denver Post, did a special political profile on the two County political chairmen – Bob Lee, Republican, and Robert S. Appel, Democrat.

Bob Lee – Republican

About Lee, Gavin wrote:

"Robert E. (for Erwin) Lee is the energetic chairman of the Republican Party in Denver. He's about the closest thing to a pro – in the sense of hard eyed knowledgeability, not play for pay – in Denver political circles.

"Lee, although it hasn't been widely acknowledged, is one of the men who put the grand (as in impressive) back in the Grand Old Party in Colorado. That's not a claim Lee would make for himself. He might even debate it sharply, given a chance. But the graying, crew-cut Lee six years ago managed to get a quiet hold on what was then an almost somnambulant Denver Republican organization – and he's been shaking the lethargy out of it ever since.

"He was a shadowy backstage force, too, in 1960 maneuvering which took control of the state party organization from Old Guard hands and made Jean K. Tool, then a virtual unknown, Colorado GOP chairman. . . There's no sign reading Robert E. Lee, Party Ramrod, on the door to the Shirley-Savoy Hotel headquarters of the

Denver County Republican Central Committee. But there should be. The office is unmistakably Lee's lair. . .

"Bob Lee gets a tense look, sort of like a minister at a burlesque show, when asked what he's done since becoming county GOP chairman to improve the party organization.

"He has no intention, he makes it clear, of estranging any former party powers by unfavorable comparisons between the way they and he operate. . .

"As organization head, Lee:

- Switched the county GOP headquarters from a seasonal campaign cranny to a year-round office.
- Named a party treasurer and placed all finances on a regularly audited basis.
- Established a needed party understructure which divided the city into 12 areas, each with a GOP lieutenant responsible for keeping lines of communication open between headquarters and three of the city's 36 election districts.
- Launched a long campaign to eliminate dead timber in the party's district and precinct organizations. . .

"By and large he's succeeded. . .Of Republicans' 72 district captains, only 16 had those positions when Lee began to slowly remold the party in 1956. And those 16, party observers say, are both interested and energetic. . .

"Probably most symptomatic of Denver GOP organizational health is the party block worker set up. . .

"'We've got 'em,' Lee says. 'You see that card file? There's 10,000 names in that file, and every one of them worked on the Nixon campaign in '60.'

"Two years ago there were 44,232 more registered Democrats in Denver than Republicans. But GOP presidential candidate Richard M. Nixon came out of the general elections with only 191 fewer votes than the Democrats' John F. Kennedy. . .

"Speaking in what obviously are personal maxims, Lee says:

- An informed group of workers will work twice as hard.

- Active Republicanism is an expanding thing. They talk about the party and its candidates everywhere – at their bridge clubs, in beauty parlors, at social gatherings.

"Of his block worker program, Lee says:

'When we're finished we can pick any block in Denver and have a pretty good idea what will happen there in the election.'

"Lee has a let's-not-horse-around approach to politics. Where the state GOP has a much-lauded loose-leaf precinct worker's manual which is a masterpiece of cartoon illustrations and printing, Lee uses a single sheet of mimeographed information. In just 41 typewritten lines it spells out the neighborhood worker's role. . .

"He expects developing party muscle to win additional Denver legislative seats and perhaps, mean the difference this fall in whether the GOP or Democrats control the State House of Representatives. Denver Republicans now hold only one of the city's eight Senate seats and three of the 17 in the House. Two years ago, though, they were shut out completely.

"What sort of Republican is Robert E. Lee . . . liberal, middle-road or conservative? When he bucked the Party's Old Guard most onlookers presumed he was if not liberal, at least a Young Turk sort. That feeling was renewed when he became a strong factor in Jean Tool's successful challenge of party mossbacks for the state organization chairmanship.

"He'd given most party candidates a bad case of muttering insomnia in 1958, though, when he led GOP captains into a public endorsement of the touchy (and later defeated) "right to work" amendment. . .

"Probably the best appraisal of the type of Republican Robert Erwin Lee is would be another word entirely: ENERGETIC."

Tom Gavin's other Political Profile was similarly detailed about Robert S. Appel, a young (36) Denver attorney who was practicing in the law firm his late father, Walter M., founded with another well-known attorney, Ira Rothberger. Gavin writes:

"Stand him up in front of the city's 914 Democratic precinct committeemen and women, a sometimes carnivorous group, and he has the appearance of a freshman theology student who flunked the

48

class in the pulpit poise. But, if pressed, Appel can use the chairman's gavel and party rule book as Claude Beatty does a whip in a cage full of Bengals. He can be as forceful as almost any occasion necessitates."

Bob Appel – Democrat

Bob Lee and Bob Appel were friends; both operated out of the Shirley-Savoy Hotel; and it was not uncommon to see them having a drink at the Hotel's bar late at night after respective political work.

The friendship was based on mutual admiration, not political philosophy. They both knew that come 1962 Appel would be working to re-elect Governor McNichols and Bob was preparing for the election of a Republican Governor – whoever the candidate might be.

Chapter 6

Robert E. Lee – 1962

LOVE
CONQUERS ALL

Who discovered John A. Love, the political novice who upset incumbent Steven L. R. McNichols in the race for Governor in 1962? The answer depends on whom you ask. Many claim the honor and there is some dispute as to the true story. However, there is no question but that Bob Lee, Denver County GOP Chairman, and his counterpart at the state level, Jean K. Tool, rejuvenated a tired Republican Party that united behind Love and won the Governor's office.

To win a statewide election, Lee had to increase Republican strength in Denver and other large Colorado counties. In 1961 he instituted a series of monthly meetings of the Republican Chairmen of the 10 largest populated counties, with the assistance of retired Army Colonel Paul Wolf, Lee's counterpart in Arapahoe County. Regular attendees included: Chuck Taylor, a CPA, Adams County; Joe Dolan, attorney, Boulder County; Weldon Tarter, attorney, El Paso County; Tom Carney, attorney, Jefferson County; Ron Strahle, attorney, Larimer County; Chuck Lumley, attorney, Mesa County; Joe Vento, attorney, Pueblo County; and Sam Telep, attorney, Weld County. Bill Seielstad, former Denverite and real estate entrepreneur from Archuleta County; Jackson Clark, owner of a hardware store in La Plata County in Durango; and Bud Hover, another former Denverite who was County Chairman in Douglas County also attended the meetings usually held in the University Club in Downtown Denver.

Tool, former County Chairman of Arapahoe County and now State Chairman, attended some of the meetings. Usually, the County Chairmen would bring one or more of their lieutenants with them.

Lee set the agenda for the group: 1. Beat McNichols; 2. Elect a Republican majority in the State House and Senate; and 3. Defeat incumbent U. S. Senator and Democrat from Denver, John Carroll.

Potential candidates for the various elective offices, especially for Governor, were discussed at length. The first name to surface was Donald G. Brotzman. Don had become involved in Republican politics shortly after graduating from the University of Colorado in 1949 with a B.S. degree as well as a Juris Doctorate. Like Bob Lee, Brotzman had been a scholar and an athlete in college. He was all conference in football, lettered in track as a shot putter and discus thrower, and was elected to Sumalia, a men's honorary society, and served on the Law Review Board.

"In 1950 I joined Vergyl Reynolds' law firm," Brotzman remembers. "Vergyl was GOP County Chairman which gave me an opportunity to observe the political process and whetted my appetite to give Boulder County better representation in the Colorado General Assembly."

"Brotz" was elected to the Colorado House of Representatives in 1950 and at the end of his first term, was selected as outstanding freshman legislator in the House by the press. In 1952 he was elected to the Colorado Senate for a four-year term and again was named by the press as the "outstanding freshman senator."

He was now 32 years old and became the nominee for the Republican Party for Governor running against Senator Ed Johnson, a former Governor, Lieutenant Governor and three times United States Senator. "I carried a majority of the counties, but could not surmount the overwhelming Democratic registration in Denver and Pueblo," Brotzman said. "The same factor kept me from defeating Steve McNichols in 1956 when I carried more counties than McNichols, but still lost due to Denver and Pueblo."

While Brotzman was debating whether or not to try again for the governorship, Lee and his cohorts were talking about other possible candidates. Brotzman finally decided to run for the United States House of Representatives and was elected in 1962 to the 88th Congress. In 1964 he lost the seat to Roy McVickers but came back in 1966 and re-won the seat for the Republican Party. He beat McVickers again in 1968, Richard Gebhart in 1970, and Francis Brush in 1972.

"The coverup of the breakin at the Democratic National Headquarters at Watergate resulted in Nixon resigning his office on August 9, 1974," Brotzman said. "The whole event had serious political repercussions for President Gerald Ford and other Republicans resulting in my defeat by Tim Wirth."

During the discussions of possible gubernatorial candidates, a new name came up – John A. Love, a young lawyer from Colorado Springs. There are stories that circulate among Republican regulars, about who discovered John Love.

Jim Aspinwall, who worked with Bob Lee in real estate as well as many political campaigns, recalls going to Colorado Springs with Bob and meeting with John Love and his wife, Ann. "We sat in the living room of their home with both John and Ann," Aspinwall said. "As I remember, Bob wanted to make sure that Love was a solid conservative Republican and wanted him to promise that he would work with Republican leadership throughout the campaign." He also recalled that Ann took exception when either he or Bob, in an offhand remark, indicated John would be a good politician. Ann objected saying, "Don't call John a politician – he's an honest man."

Love, during an interview for this book, when asked who had "discovered" him said, "Frankly, I don't know." Then he added, "I always wanted to be in public life, but I wanted to be in a position of having enough money so that I would not be totally dependent on politics for my livelihood. My intent really was to run for Congress and I called on the incumbent, Judge Edgar Chenoweth, but he told me he didn't intend to retire. So, actually, I started thinking about running for Governor simply to get name recognition so that I could eventually run for Congress."

Love admitted he had no political experience and had never run for an elective office except, "I did run against Weldon Tarter for County Chairman of El Paso County and only lost by one vote."

A good friend of Love's, Harry Hart of Colorado Springs,(later, one of Love's Administrative Assistants and a State Representative) deserves some credit for the "discovery." Harry knew about the group of County Chairmen meeting regularly in Denver and brought Love to meet with Bob Lee and Ralph Clark in County headquarters, hoping Love would soon be invited to meet with other County Chairmen.

Ralph Clark, a close friend of Bob Lee and Secretary of the Republican Party in Denver, recalls: "Both Bob and I immediately asked him why he thought he could beat McNichols," Clark recalls. "Because who could be against Love?" Love responded.

Chuck Taylor, County GOP Chairman of Adams County recalled: "Brotzman straddled the fence so long, he had a crease in the seat of his pants."

After Brotzman finally told Bob and Ralph that he would not run again for Governor, but would run for Congress, Bob quickly invited John Love to meet with the County Chairmen organization that Bob had put together.

At the next University Club meeting, the group was impressed with Love's quick wit and his appearance. He was tall and handsome – some likened him to the actor, William Holden – and he had a rich baritone voice.

About this time, another well known and respected Republican, David Hamil, emerged as a candidate. Hamil, a life-long resident of Sterling, formerly represented the northeast area of Colorado in the House. He was a capable legislator and popular with his fellow legislators. House members elected him Speaker of the House in 1949. The Speaker's position is the most powerful in the House and appoints chairs of all the committees. After Dwight Eisenhower was elected President, Hamil was appointed Administrator of the Rural Electric Association, headquartered in Washington, D.C.

So Hamil was out of the state while Lee, and other new leaders, were reshaping the Republican Party.

At another meeting of the County Chairmen, Weldon Tarter of Colorado Springs speaking in favor of Love said "I'd like to get John out of El Paso County since I only beat him by one vote."

The Chairmen agreed that Love was an electable candidate. Lee, Ralph Clark and Jim Aspinwall immediately went to work rounding up votes for Love at the upcoming Republican assemblies. Lee contacted Eddie Nicholson and started a fund-raising campaign that eventually raised the $100,000 needed for the Love campaign. Clark set up Love campaign headquarters in the Shirley-Savoy Hotel, just above Bob's County GOP headquarters.

Love was not concerned about the candidacy of Dave Hamil and believed he could win the race after Brotzman eventually decided not to run. "Dave Hamil never heard of me and I never heard of him," Love recalls. "The timing was great because there was nobody but Davey Hamil and he was not a strong candidate because he had been out of the state for awhile and his role in the House as Speaker had made a lot of people unhappy. He must have wondered where in the hell I came from."

The two met at State Republican headquarters, also in the Shirley-Savoy Hotel and Love recalls Hamil standing up before the group and defending his record as a House member and House Speaker, even though he made some enemies, saying, "They say I have scars, but I want you to know that I got them representing you."

During the interview with Love in his Cherry Creek office, the former Governor pointed to a key on his memento shelf saying, "When the Shirley-Savoy Hotel was torn down, the key to my campaign headquarters room was presented to me."

Love recalled that Tom Carney nominated him for Governor at the GOP State Convention in Boulder. "Here is an interesting little story about the Convention," Love said. "During the proceedings I got very tired and went up to my room to take a little nap. As I was coming back I heard my name called, so I immediately ran down the aisle as fast as I could. It turned out that was a good thing to do because everyone figured I was young and vigorous and Dave, of course, was a few years older."

Love and Hamil gained sufficient votes at the Convention to force a primary contest on Tuesday, September 11, 1962. Gail H.

Gilbert, a former Mayor of Arvada and a veterinarian, well known for his "Dr. John" radio shows about pets, was nominated to run for Lieutenant Governor. Peter H. Dominick was the Party's choice to run against John Carroll for the United States Senate.

Love recalled the campaign with fondness: "We ran a civil, gentle primary," Love said. "I remember at one meeting where I stood up and said there was a nasty rumor being circulated that I wanted to put a stop to right now. The rumor is that Hamil was against Love. I said I had talked to Jan (Hamil's wife) and she said that's not so." (After winning the Governor's job, one of the first appointments Love made was that of Dave Hamil as Director of State Institutions.)

Love said Bob Lee and Ralph Clark directed his campaign, and Jim Aspinwall, Bud Hover and others were assigned to travel with him and maintain his schedule.

In the September primary Love won the nomination by a vote of 66,027 to 44,693 for Hamil. Peter Dominick, unopposed, received 93,802 votes. On the Democratic side, Governor Steve McNichols, unopposed, received 69,435 votes. Senator John Carroll received 76,002 votes as his party's standard bearer.

In the 1962 election each party nominated a candidate for Lieutenant Governor and they ran independently from the Governor. Gail Gilbert ended up with 87,603 votes to be the Republican candidate and Robert L. Knous, son of the former Governor, Lee Knous, attracted 72,631 votes to become the Democratic candidate for Lieutenant Governor.

Lee and Clark tagged Governor McNichols as the "big tax and spend governor," a theme that Love pounded time and time again during the campaign. "I remember Sonny Mapelli (Denver Councilman and candidate for Mayor) meeting me on the street one day and saying what a strange campaign it was," Love said. "Sonny recalled that Steve would get up on the platform and talk about government and what government was going to do and I would get up there and say only that I was going to cut taxes."

Lee's strategy was to have John sell himself to the voters as a nice guy. "I remember walking down 17th Street and was pleased when someone recognized me and came up and said, 'You're John Love and I am going to vote for you,'" Love said, "and I thanked him for that and he immediately responded, saying, 'By the way, I left my wallet at home. Could you let me have $10?'"

Ann Love was John's almost constant companion on the campaign trail, even though she did not enjoy being the wife of a political candidate and generally had a rather low opinion of professional politicians.

In response to a direct question if Mrs. Love had had a falling out with Ralph Clark, the Governor replied: "I don't recall specifically what it was, but she didn't have a lot of use for Ralph, and to some extent Bob Lee. I think it was mostly because they were running my life. When I first confided in her that I was going to run for public office, she was less than positive and told me to think twice about getting into politics because that was dirty business."

Ralph Clark recalled: "We were having a GOP event on the mezzanine of the Cosmopolitan Hotel late in the general campaign. We had been working twelve hour days for John. Ann came up to me, pointed her finger at my face, and said, 'You are killing my husband!' I told her to go home and take care of the pots and pans and we'll elect John as Governor." From that time on, Ann disliked Ralph and those, including Bob, who were directing John's campaign. Ralph, interviewed for this book, reminisced: "I was young and impetuous at the time. And also angry. All of us were working long hours at no pay to get her husband elected Governor. I learned that before I took on any other campaigns, and I've run quite a few, that I had to meet the candidate's wife before I went to work so as to determine if we were on the same team." Ralph also recalled that Bob Lee told him that after that confrontation at the Cosmopolitan Hotel, Jean Tool and Lyle Lindesmith met with Bob and told him to "get rid of Ralph." Ralph said that Bob reported that he told Tool and Lindesmith "That's not going to happen." And it didn't.

Ralph also recalled how he and Bob Rosenheim were writing daily potential press releases to be used against Governor McNichols. The drafts were taken to Jean Tool as State Chairman for review. After discovering that Jean didn't really care for the hard ball releases that Clark and Rosenheim wanted disseminated to the media, Ralph hired Jack Gaskie, a Rocky Mountain News reporter, to help disseminate the releases to the media which kept McNichols on the defensive and allowed John to steer clear of debating McNichols.

Bud Hover, who was one of the drivers assigned by Clark to get John to his scheduled events, recalled: "I drove John to a noon meeting in Weld County which Governor McNichols also attended. After the meeting, John seemed to appear weak, almost sick. I called Clark and asked him what I should do. Ralph said to put John in the back seat; drive carefully back to Denver; take him to the DAC; see that he was taken to a room there and let him take a nap. After this was done, I was to call Ralph again. He told me to get John a drink, have him take a shower, change clothes, and move on to a night meeting."

Love confirmed that he and Bob Lee were never truly close friends and did not meet socially but had a mutual respect for the role each was playing in the campaign.

"I think the Bobs – and there are not too many of them in this world – are the actual part that makes this democracy work," Love said during the interview. "And sometimes you think it's not too good for this country that these campaign managers are directing strategy. But remember, these campaign managers and chairpeople were not paid in those days. Lee was not a paid hand. And that's an important thing to know about him. He truly was a patriot and he was imbued with what we should all be imbued with, how necessary it is to participate to make the thing work."

Gail Gilbert played an important part in the campaign even though his own candidacy for Lieutenant Governor proved to be unsuccessful.

Tom Carney recalls: "Gail had a pretty good political background with a little controversy thrown in. Gail talked to me about running for Lieutenant Governor. I sent him off to see Bob.

"When Bob called about Gilbert, I told him Gail could be an attack dog if that's what we wanted. He had no scandal in his background but could be controversial. Bob ran Gail around to the other Chairmen, and we ended up with a Lieutenant Governor candidate.

"During the campaign Lee (with accord by others of us) gave Gilbert the task of attacking Governor McNichols. Love's function was to look like a Governor. I think everyone thought that if Love won, Gilbert would ride his coattails to victory. We were wrong. Everyone won except Gilbert. To this day he thinks we, Lee included, let him down. Perhaps we did, but it was a miscalculation rather than anything else.

"Throughout the Love campaign, Lee called the shots. His people were in the office, handled the press and coordinated John's activities, raised his campaign funds and established the tenor of the campaign."

Gail Gilbert remembers meeting Bob Lee before his campaign for Lieutenant Governor and doesn't believe the Party let him down. "I remember in late 1961 visiting the Denver Republican Party headquarters in the Shirley-Savoy Hotel," Gilbert said. "The offices of the Party were hardly elegant but it was immediately evident who was the boss. The office of Bob Lee was the best equipped of all.

"Bob met me with good grace and courtesy and I was surprised that he knew so much about me. He was not effusive nor the least overbearing as might befit an officer of his political power. He set me down and made me completely at ease. I asked him to support my candidacy for Lieutenant Governor. He supported my candidacy without any hesitation or exceptions. Later I came to realize that the word given by Bob Lee was his bond.

"During the Convention in Boulder, Bob was confronted by a West Slope politician who demanded vociferously that Bob take his support of me and give it to another potential candidate. This argument nearly reached a physical standoff. Bob never gave an inch. He stood by his word and I came out of that Convention with a towering majority, all due to one Bob Lee.

"The fact that I did not win the election in the fall was not Bob Lee's fault. In spite of my personal loss in this political effort, I gained so much more by winning Bob Lee's friendship.

"He, in my opinion, will always be one of the giants of Republican politics in Colorado and he will forever occupy a large space in my heart."

The strategy of attacking the incumbent Governor as "big tax and spend McNichols," coupled with Love's concentration on selling himself paid off. Also, there were hundreds of billboards and bus

Governor John Love

signs and yard signs, all saying "Love for Colorado." And the voters responded.

In one of the biggest upsets in modern Colorado political history, Love easily ousted McNichols. The statewide vote was Love 349,342; McNichols 262,890; a majority of 86,452 votes. (Four years earlier, McNichols had beaten the Republican candidate Burch by 92,522 votes – 321,165 to 228,643.)

Even more striking was Love's showing in typical Democratic areas. He pulled 88,087 votes in Denver to McNichols' 87,754; Pueblo: Love 23,302 – McNichols 17,326; Adams County: Love 16,593; – McNichols 16,440; Boulder: Love 16,756 – McNichols 11,495.

Before the final vote, Lee had confided to his associates that he was convinced that Love was far ahead and that Peter Dominick needed more help. As a result, Lee and his workers concentrated on the senatorial election with the following results: Dominick 328,655 – incumbent Senator John Carroll 279,586.

Knous was one of the few Democrats who survived the Republican landslide. He defeated Gilbert 303,359 votes to 292,401. Both the House and Senate went Republican.

There is an old military maxim that "to the victor go the spoils." This also applies to politics, generally. But not in the case of the strong supporters of Love who expected some patronage. They were to receive none from the newly elected Governor.

Chapter 7

Bee, Delisa, Bob

FEUDING, FUSSING AND RESIGNATION

"After the classic Republican victory in 1962, I began ever so slowly to learn the truth of an old political adage: Victory is far harder to manage than defeat."

These are the words of Jean Tool, State GOP Chairman who worked with Bob Lee and Bob's County Chairmen organization guiding John Love to his upset victory over the incumbent, Steve McNichols, in the 1962 Governor's race.

That was November 6. On December 12, 1962, Bob Lee announced his resignation as Chairman of the Denver Republican Party, effective January 1. Whether or not there was any connection between Lee's resignation and Love's failure to appoint any of Lee's lieutenants to state government posts is a matter of speculation.

"I think generally my wife, Ann, had sort of a resentment feeling that Bob was trying to run my governorship," Love said. "I don't know whether I was upset about it particularly, but I appointed Lindy (Lyle Lindesmith) as Chief of Staff and he was somewhat anti-Lee. Well, I felt a little tinge of guilt in that as much as Bob had done, that I didn't reward him. But it didn't seem right to me that that's what you did in politics – reward. I was that naive. But I had to make a declaration of independence."

Tool believes the Governor was fair to all segments of the party in the appointments he made.

"After John Love's inauguration as Governor, the good hard-working leadership which had done so much to modernize the GOP in Denver County began to want to collect some of their chips," Tool remembers. "Frankly, these fellows saw all their chips through blue-tinted glasses, whereas I could count a thousand yeowomen and men in the other 62 counties who had won many chips as well. The incessant enthusiasm which took these workers to virtually every doorknob in Colorado was the ingredient which won the upset. Denver County jolly well did its bit, but it didn't come anywhere near to earning the spoils that it sought to claim over the months following the victory."

In summary, Tool said, the new Governor Love had appointed something like 140 persons to boards and commissions by the autumn of 1963. More than 90 of these were from Denver. However, not one of Bob's captains or area leaders was appointed.

Bob Rosenheim, one of Lee's top district captains for ten years, and, at Bob Lee's urging, later appointed regional director of Housing and Urban Development by President Nixon, recalls Bob's disappointment that Love, after his election, "did not appoint any of Lee's key workers to his cabinet or other administrative posts. Bob was always proud of Dick Batterton's appointment of his people and Bob was certain John would do the same, but it didn't happen, and Bob Lee never forgot, although he only talked about it with a few of us. This experience helped him later with Governor Kirk and President Nixon who did appoint key Lee workers to important administrative positions."

Jim Aspinwall remembered how much Lyle Lindesmith, who became Love's chief of staff, disliked Bob. "Having been Tool's assistant at state headquarters," Aspinwall said, "he knew who Tool's friends were and these were the people John appointed from Denver. Of Lee's handwritten list of captains and area leaders (see page 38), only Lou Middlemist was later appointed purchasing officer after the Batterton defeat of 1963 and not at Bob's request."

Love recalled that "Bobby only once asked me to appoint anyone, to the best of my knowledge. He asked me to do something for

64

Jim Aspinwall." When asked if Aspinwall was appointed to any position, he replied in the negative.

This, however, was not Lee's reason for resigning. In his personal papers, Lee stated frankly that he returned full time to his real estate office because "by this time I really needed the money." Even though there had been some speculation about Lee vacating the post, the actual resignation came as a shock to most party workers. His resignation and accolades that followed were chronicled by the press as follows:

Wednesday, December 12, 1962 *The Denver Post*, by Tom Gavin: "Robert E. Lee formally announced Tuesday night that he will resign as chairman of the Denver Republican Party Jan. 1.

"Lee confirmed his resignation plan – which had been an open secret in the party for almost a month – at a testimonial dinner in his honor at the Lakewood Country Club. The outgoing GOP chairman was given a new station wagon by party associates in appreciation of efforts which brought the Denver political organization from a position of weakness to one of strength in four years.

"Among possible successors to Lee are Joseph L. Pittroff, a Denver lawyer and unsuccessful City Council candidate four years ago, and Robert C. Rosenheim, regional sales manager of the Owens-Illinois Glass Co.'s container division. Ralph M. Clark, Denver GOP secretary, said emphatically Wednesday that he has no interest in the chairmanship.

"A 10-member party committee has been named to interview chairman prospects. It hasn't been decided, though, whether an interim appointment will be made by the party organization's vacancy committee or whether the GOP Central Committee will be called into session to elect an interim chairman. Lee's current two-year term does not expire until March, when the Central Committee must meet and elect new officers.

"There have been rumors that, because of his successful Denver organizational work, the Republican National Committee has been attempting to lure Lee to a national staff job – either to help in strengthening the party in northern urban areas, or in the South. Lee, however, insists his only present interest is returning to his Denver real estate firm. His unpaid chairman's post has required virtually full time attention for most of this campaign year.

"Lee also denied speculation that he might be appointed to a state position by the incoming GOP Governor, John A. Love, and that he might seek election to public office – as that of Denver mayor – himself. 'I have absolutely no political plans at all,' he said. 'I am leaving so that – as I've always preached – we can get some new blood in the party organization.'

"Lee assumed the city party leader's job in March 1958 – a year in which the GOP organization here was so weak it was unable to elect a single Denver Republican to the Legislature. At the following 1960 general election, Republicans won one of the four Denver State Senate seats at issue and three of the 17 House seats. This year, despite the Democratic prominence in the city, two of the other four Senate seats went to Republicans and seven of the 17 House seats. The local party even won a slight majority for Love in Denver.

"In addition to the new car, Lee was presented at the surprise testimonial dinner Tuesday night with a scroll which said, 'Your efforts, more than any other person's, have been the basis for revitalization of the Republican Party in Colorado.' It was signed by all of the more than 75 persons at the dinner. Among those eulogizing the 49-year-old Lee were Jean K. Tool, the state Republican chairman, and Love, who said, 'I would not be governor-elect if it were not for Bob Lee.' Lee said he is resigning Jan. 1, rather than waiting for his full term to expire, so that the new chairman will not take office in the middle of Denver's mayoralty campaign. The municipal election will be May 21. Although city elections are nominally nonpartisan, both major parties take active parts in the campaign – on an 'unofficial' level."

From the Colorado Trumpet and Public Ledger (A Partisan Republican weekly):

"Robert E. Lee is stepping down as chairman of the Denver GOP Central Committee. Robert E. Lee's resignation deserves editorial treatment because of 63 county chairmen, he has done one of the most remarkable jobs in the state – and that's saying a lot when you consider the number of other truly outstanding chairmen of the 63

Bee, Delisa and Bob beside station wagon gift

counties. We're not sure just how we should approach Bob editori-
ally because with two exceptions, he is the epitome of everything
we detest in a county chairman:

"He is never available. When he dropped in to State HQ he either
needed a phone or went through like a cyclone with no comment.
He never had anything 'newsworthy.' Only once in two and a half
years did we have a direct quote from Bob, and that was because he
sent out a press release. (On the opposite side, he would refer us to
Billie Briggs, Denver vice chairman, and fortunately for us, Billie
had news.) He never seemed to do anything. It was always someone
else who did it. We knew better, but what do you do with a guy who
comes around acting lazy and relaxed and seldom even talked politics? Other chairmen didn't do anything either, but they told us who
did.

"On the other hand, Bob Lee is a heck of a nice guy. He also has
the know-how to build a county organization into a winning one. A

GOP win for Denver is a plum. In the first place, Democrats out register Republicans by a considerable number. In the second place, if a candidate loses by a heavy margin in Denver it takes a miracle in 62 other counties to bring through a winner. GOP state candidates have lost in Denver and won an election, but it required a heavy GOP vote to do so. For instance, Gordon Allott lost Denver by 1,000 votes in 1960; Peter Dominick lost it by 2,000 this year. John Love, however, carried Denver by 313 while Lt. Gov. Bob Knous held a margin of 18,000 – and that's a margin hard to make up. Winning helps, of course, but when you've got miserable odds it's a tremendous feat to rally the troops to hold a workable margin.

"The real positive proof of Bob's pudding is in the state legislature where not one GOP incumbent was defeated and Denver gained four House seats and two Senate seats. The proof is also in the Denver party organization which has one of the finest group of dedicated blockworkers (8,000 of them) in the state. (This is the 'someone else' who does the work Bob won't admit to, although there seems to be a void in explaining how the blockworkers got lined up.)

"What many people do not realize is the complexity of the Denver GOP organization. There are 36 districts – each captained by one woman and one man – in the city. Under them comes the precinct committee people and blockworkers. The Denver county chairman rides herd on these 72 captains – many of whom head districts larger than some of Colorado's counties voter-wise. If the captains don't operate, the entire structure could collapse. The Denver chairman has to keep the structure solid if he has to hold it up himself. There have been times when Bob Lee has done just that. Denver county is a well organized, well operated and highly successful operation. Ask any political observer why, and they tell you, 'because of Bob Lee.'"

But Bob was addicted to politics and would not remain inactive for long, even though he resigned his chairmanship.

"Bob gained a great deal of recognition because of this campaign," Governor Love said. "The recognition was nationwide and I believe that's why the national organization called on him for help in New Jersey and Florida."

Chapter 8

A POLITICAL SANDWICH: NEW JERSEY AND FLORIDA WITH COLORADO IN BETWEEN

Lee in Florida – 1966

Governor Love was correct. His upset over incumbent Democratic Governor Steven L. R. McNichols had been duly noted at national Republican Party headquarters. And officials were well aware of Bob Lee's work in that victory. Jean Tool, who also played a key role in Love's election as Republican Party State Chairman, recalls:

"In the winter of 1962-63 at the regular National Republican Committee meeting in Washington, we Coloradans were the lions of the meeting because the 1962 Republican sweep here exceeded the quality and depth of any other victory in any other state."

His "reward" for that victory, Tool said, was that he was named to the site selection committee for the 1964 Republican National Convention. (Tool also was called to assist Winthrop Rockefeller in his unsuccessful campaign for governor in Arkansas.)

Lee's "reward" was a request by party officials to elect a Republican to the New Jersey Senate from a district and a state that was controlled by Democrats.

"Shortly after I resigned as chairman in January, 1963 and went back to work full time in my real estate office," Bob wrote in notes about the New Jersey sojourn, "I had a phone call from Jack Quinn,

69

a public relations man from Omaha who had done work for Nixon in 1960 in the midwestern states. Jack was very secretive but said he had a proposition to talk over with me." The proposition was to master plan the GOP campaign.

Lee recalled that his first inclination was to say no "because they only offered to pay a small sum that wouldn't cover expenses. But my curiosity started to work on me as to why Republicans could not win in big Eastern states," Bob stated. "The challenge got to me and I spent seven months in the campaign." His responsibilities, once he was on board in New Jersey, spilled over into all the legislative races.

Tool recalls talking to Web Todd, National Committeeman for New Jersey, at a cocktail party during the Republican National Committee meeting in Washington. "Web asked me if anyone in Colorado would be fit to run an election campaign in Essex County (including Newark)," Tool said, "and without hesitation, I said Bob Lee." Tool admits he had another reason for recommending Lee for the job. "Even though I felt strongly that Bob's brass knuckle style, total dedication to cause and candidate, understanding of political intrigues, knowledge of the importance of door-to-door registration and vote recruitment, and a bloodhound's instinct for where the money hides, would fit nicely in any problems in Essex County," he said, "it also was a chance to move Lee out of the State for awhile so that the disagreements between Lee and the governor about appointments could quiet down." Lee moved to New Jersey and took on the responsibility of running the campaign of C. Robert Sarcone, the minority leader in the New Jersey House, in his bid to win the Senate seat from his district which was held by a Democrat. In a telephone interview with the author in August of 1998, Sarcone said he told the Party he would run but that he needed help and didn't have any money to pay for it. "The State Chairman, Web Todd, said he had lined up a real pro from Colorado who had just gotten an unknown candidate elected for Governor over a strong incumbent," Sarcone said. "I told him I didn't have any money to pay him and Web told me not to worry, that a company, S. & H. Green Stamps, had agreed to pick up the tab."

Sarcone recalled that he was surprised when he first met Lee. "He wasn't very big, and he smoked almost continuously," Sarcone said, "but we had a long meeting about what had to be done to beat the Democrats. And we worked well together during the campaign."

Jack Wogan, who later served as Chairman of the Republican Party in Denver, spent a few days with Lee in New Jersey and remembered, "When Bobby went to New Jersey he was on unknown turf. Republicans caucused in a phone booth, and Democrats owned the north New Jersey establishment, the union halls and usually the election process. Bobby put in unbelievable hours, organizing block workers, attending meetings, learning the local issues, discussing these with contributors, and, most important, meeting with reporters because the war was going to be won or lost in the newspapers."

Lee obviously impressed the press. Maurice C. Carroll, a writer for the New York Herald Tribune, published a story on October 27, 1963, just before the election. A shortened version of the story, which captures Lee's personality and sets forth in some detail his philosophy, his dedication, and his work habits, follows:

"NEWARK, N.J. The sun turned the smog into a glimmering haze and from half a block away, you could barely make out the 'Sarcone for Senator' banner that dangled from the Military Park Hotel.

"Robert Lee's eyes watered, 'I'm a mountaineer,' he boomed. 'I don't know how long it takes you to get used to this.' Smog is just about the only thing here that has defied Mr. Lee's determined efforts at total comprehension. He came in from Denver August 1, a man with a mission, and by now he could stick a pin in the map of Essex County and hit a Republican voter. 'You know,' he said gleefully a few minutes later over a cup of coffee, 'you know, we might just be able to win this.'

"A crew cut bantam, with a booming outdoors voice, Mr. Lee said he came here because 'Bob Sarcone called me on the telephone and asked me to' and he jabbed at the air with his cigarette and said firmly that on the day after election, he and his wife will drive back home to Colorado and he'll tend to things political there and nowhere else.

". . . Why is he here in New Jersey's biggest city? He's learning what the Republican Party can do to diminish the massive tide of Democratic votes that pours forth from most of the nation's big cities. Mr. Lee leaned forward and his eyes narrowed thoughtfully. 'The Republican Party has an inherent problem,' he said slowly, 'most of its members are middle class. There are few of what you would call political professionals. They can get stirred up every four years, but that's not how this thing works – you have to have the horses trained and ready to go for every single race.'

"Does he really believe Republicans can carry the big cities? 'No, but we can cut 'em down. In 1960 Nixon went out of the city of Denver just 325 votes behind Kennedy and we carried the state easily. Take here. There are special factors, of course: there always are in every election. This Bob Sarcone is a real tiger, the opposition has made some bad mistakes, there's a split-off group of Democrats (he was talking about a ticket headed by a Negro Assemblyman, George Richardson) that is going to gobble up some minority group voices. But everyone is working and you're not going to see one of those 40,000 vote Democratic margins in Newark this time or I'll buy you a hat.'

"In the well-to-do Essex suburbs, the citizens emerge from their split levels and vote overwhelmingly Republican so that if Mr. Lee's hold-the-line prediction bears up in Newark, his man could win. Other than placing another Republican in office, would this mean much for the national party? 'Well, first, you have to understand that there are no magic gimmicks in this city or any place else. It's all people. You have to be patient, make sure you pick the right ones, train 'em, keep working. A political organization is not like a machine – it's like a sales organization, and you have to line up effective salesmen.'

"And how will these lessons be transmitted? Mr. Lee grinned. 'Denver is a sort of communication center. You might say that I'm in occasional contact with other chairmen around the west.'

"From time to time during the conversation the names of former GOP chairman Leonard Hall and former Vice President Richard M. Nixon came up and they elicited a glow of admiration from Mr. Lee that might indicate his course. 'Richard Nixon? What would I do to help elect him president? Anything he asked.'"

Tool recalls visiting Bob in New Jersey in October of 1963 while he was seeking accounts for his advertising agency in New York City. "I called Bob and invited myself over for dinner," Tool recalls. "Bob was very enthusiastic about the campaign."

Lee called on another Colorado friend, Congressman Don Brotzman, and asked him to come to New Jersey and give a pep talk to Bob's female volunteers. Brotzman later said it was his very best upbeat speech and indicated Bob felt it helped his efforts tremendously, "particularly to get block workers in the Senate District working full time."

The election results exceeded even the most optimistic Republican hopes. Not only was Sarcone elected 125,836 votes to 109,934 votes for the Democratic candidate, Homer Matthews, but the Republicans won control of the Senate by a majority of five and, most surprisingly, captured control of the lower House.

LATE SPORTS
WALL STREET
★★★★★★
Financial News, Pages 40, 41

Newark Evening News

RACE RESULTS
SPORTS FINAL
★★★★★★
Rain tonight, partly cloudy tomorrow.

No. 24,660   NEWARK, N.J., WEDNESDAY, NOVEMBER 6, 1963   TELEPHONE MARKET 4-1000 ★ ★ ★ ★   SEVEN CENTS

Bond Issue Crushed

Sarcone Runaway Helps GOP Win Assembly

Stamler Also In

Senate Is 15-6; House Stands 33 to 27

By ANGELO BAGLIVO

Spearheaded by the victory of Assemblyman C. Robert Sarcone in the Essex County senatorial race, New Jersey Republicans yesterday captured control of the Assembly for the first time in six years and strengthened their Senate majority by four.

The Republican victory took 11 Assembly seats now held by Democrats in Essex, Union, Camden and Burlington Counties, giving the GOP control of the House by 33-27. In '961, the Democrats won 38 seats to 22 for the Republicans.

The four Senate seats taken from the Democrats swelled the Republican majority to a commanding 15-6. The Republican Senate majority now is 11-10.

The election results will confront Gov. Hughes next year with both houses of the Legislature controlled by the opposition party — adding another bitter blow on top of defeat of the governor's $750 million bond issue referendum.

HAPPY FAMILY—Assembly Minority Leader C. Robert Sarcone, Essex senator-elect, is all smiles as are his wife, Jeanette (at right) and their daughter Yvonne, 11.

Essex GOP Wins Senate, 5 Assembly, 2 County Posts

Newark Evening News

73

Lee, despite his frantic time schedule in New Jersey, found time to visit family and friends in Denver and survey the political scene. Things were not going well for the Denver Republican Party. The incumbent Republican Mayor, Richard Batterton, was being challenged for that office by Thomas G. Currigan, who was completing his second four-year term as elected City Auditor. Batterton had announced his candidacy for reelection on February 22, 1963.

As George Kelly recounts in his book detailing races of mayors in Denver, "Bob Lee was back on the scene for Batterton and a relative newcomer to Democratic politics, Vincent Ryan, directed the Currigan campaign." Both newspapers favored a third candidate, attorney William W. Grant, a Democrat, with a family name well known in Denver political and social circles. The Denver Post, particularly its publisher, Palmer Hoyt, was disenchanted with Batterton as Mayor and dismissed the incumbent auditor as a serious candidate.

Batterton's bid for reelection was seriously undermined because of the scandal in the Denver Police Department which resulted in scores of officers being tried, convicted and sent to prison for burglary. Batterton had downplayed the seriousness of the problem, claiming Denver had one of the nation's finest police forces and that "in any group of 750 people you are likely to turn up a bad apple or two." That quote came back to haunt him through the campaign.

Lee did what he could to distance Batterton from that scandal by linking Currigan with James Hoffa, International Teamster's Union president. In an interview, Lee had stated that Bobby Whaley, a former patrolman serving a burglary sentence, was a police union official and had ties with the Teamsters. Currigan responded that police should have the privilege of joining the union if they wished – prompting Lee's remarks about Hoffa.

Grant was eliminated in the May primary. In the June election, Currigan was elected with 72,848 votes to Batterton's 58,153.

While Batterton was losing his bid for reelection, Lee's successor as County Chairman, L. Joseph Pittroff, developed health problems, and resigned the position in July. One faction in the party wanted Lee to return to the chairmanship and another supported

Jerry McHugh, the party secretary. Lee won the election in September by a vote of 395 to 276, with John D. Wogan, Jr. elected secretary. The County party's Vice Chairman, Mrs. Billie Briggs, a McHugh supporter, resigned and later at a special election, Mrs. Helen Johnson was elected Vice Chairman without opposition.

While this division within the Denver GOP was being resolved, another surfaced at the state level – who would be the Party's national committeeman? On June 4, 1964, Dan Thomasson, reported in the Rocky Mountain News:

"Denver Republican District Captains lined up solidly Wednesday behind County Chairman Robert E. Lee in the party fratricidal national committeeman fight.

"In an emergency meeting called by Denver Vice Chairman, Helen Johnson, they endorsed Lee, his policies and his candidacy . . . in all, 75 persons signed a resolution praising Lee's ability and personal sacrifice as the party Chairman throughout the years . . . the resolution stated that Lee had agreed to run again for county chairman last September only after he had repeatedly been urged to do so by Republican captains and committee people. . . The meeting, conducted at County headquarters in the Park Lane Hotel, obviously was an outgrowth of recent attacks on Lee by supporters of National Committeeman William Powers. . . Lee is backing oilman John King of Denver for Powers' National Committee post.

"Powers, with the help of Senators Dominick, Allott and Governor Love, was reelected National Committeeman. Lee then urged the three top elected Republican officials to 'assume some of the dirt that goes along with party leadership.'"

Lee was quoted in newspapers as saying, "The leadership assumed by the three at the two-day Republican Convention that led to Powers' election could be healthy. But with that leadership goes some of the responsibility of the organization such as helping to raise money, recruiting membership and pushing Party functions." Lee congratulated Powers and told him "the thing to do now is to win the election in November."

However, their efforts and Lee's, who was a strong Goldwater supporter, were of little use as Lyndon Johnson won the election by a landslide over Barry Goldwater. In February, 1965, Lee, Johnson and Wogan were elected to their party positions without opposition. After this election, Lee appointed Bruce Dines Treasurer, Phil Pankey, finance chairman and John Law, legal advisor.

Lee continued in that post and plied his real estate trade in Denver until March, 1966, when he again resigned the position. The reason? The Republican Party needed help in Florida.

Lee's friend, Edward Nicholson, had retired and was living in Fort Lauderdale, Florida. Nicholson met with Florida GOP leaders and Leonard Hall, former Republican national chairman and talked about the possibility of electing a Republican governor in Florida. Lee received a telephone call from Nicholson and Hall.

"They told me there was a man named Claude Kirk, who had filed to run for governor of Florida," Lee recalled in his memoirs. "They said he had asked them to help him get someone who could set up and successfully manage his campaign and they wanted me to come to Florida and talk with him. I argued against it, but these two men had helped me politically when I needed them so to keep the peace I finally agreed to go down for four days and at least meet Kirk."

Kirk was a Marine Corps veteran and graduate of the University of Alabama Law School. He became a resident of Florida when he turned the American Heritage Insurance Company into a highly successful and prosperous company. He then became involved in investment banking – and politics. In 1960 he headed the Democrats for Nixon organization in Florida.

In his book, *Claude Kirk and the Politics of Confrontation*, Edmund F. Kallina, Jr., the author noted that "Kirk had no desire to work his way up through the political ranks. He preferred to start at the top of Florida. The Republican Party organization was moribund and did almost no campaigning except in presidential contests. Few individuals were brash enough to run for office as a Republican.

"But Kirk was. In 1964, despite the fact that he had never held public office nor even run for office, he became the Republican nominee for the U. S. Senate." That seat was held by a Governor and three-term Senator, Spencer Holland,, who walloped Kirk in the election by over 100,000 votes. Even so, Republicans in Florida were impressed because Kirk had managed to get 562,000 votes.

This helped Kirk not only to raise campaign funds, but brought him to the attention of the National GOP. And such leaders as Nicholson and Leonard Hall. Thus, the call to Bob Lee.

Kirk was a maverick from the beginning to the end of his political career – switching parties and defying established party leaders. But he was charming and humorous, a brilliant speaker and a gifted story teller who possessed an extraordinary memory. And he was a conservative. Lee took on the job of managing his campaign, even though he knew little of Florida and less about Florida politics.

Lee recounted his first meeting with Kirk: "Our meeting was brief and Kirk announced that he had some appointments around the state and decided I should go with him. For four days we flew the state in a small four-passenger, single engine plane. While he was speaking in Tallahassee I spent time in the secretary of state's office gathering election laws, previous election results, registration figures and other information that might give me an insight to the potential of Kirk's candidacy.

"I watched a couple of TV interviews Kirk had with the press and was impressed with his ability to handle himself in touchy situations. But at the end of four days I was ready to return to Denver, and at that point, felt I had seen the last of Florida, although the temptation was great to explore the possibilities of a Republican winning in a deep south state."

But Kirk and national party leaders continued to call him, urging him to take on the job because they wanted to break the strangle hold the Democrats had on the "solid south." Lee called district captains in Denver and told them of his decision and it was decided that Jack Wogan, party secretary, should be the new Chairman. Lee determined that Kirk would have no difficulty in winning the primary contest facing him in May, 1966, so he concentrated on the Democratic primary.

"Inasmuch as there were thousands of registered Democrats who were really transplanted Republicans from the North and we knew about them because they had contributed and helped in previous elections," Lee recounted, "we put on a campaign to get them to go in and vote for Robert King High, the Mayor of Miami, one of three Democratic candidates."

The GOP did this because they felt Kirk's best chance was against High who was known for his liberalism. High won the Democratic nomination setting up the race in the general election between him and Kirk. The basic theme throughout the campaign was Kirk's conservatism versus High's liberalism.

From day one Lee started building a volunteer organization. He wrote, "I worked out an organization chart and broke it down to these departments. (1) Area, county and precinct organization headed up by an organization director; (2) Finance chairman to handle fund raising; (3) A treasurer (as required by state law) to handle all accounting of funds and file appropriate reports to the secretary of state's office; (4) Publicity department to handle all speed writing, media releases, advertising, advance preparation for rallies; (5) Scheduling director who was to be in complete charge of the candidate's schedule; (6) A special group chairman who would organize all groups other than on geographical lines – this would overlap the precinct organization; and (7) Research department – search out all information both past and present on our candidate and his opponent."

State campaign headquarters were established in Fort Lauderdale and Lee started setting up a precinct organization and filling his organizational chart. He convinced Carey Conry, "a great gal who had helped me for a long time, a conservative with strong convictions who was financially self sufficient to come to Florida from Denver and keep our records and set up a card file." She did. Kirk then started campaigning throughout the state, visiting the smaller counties first. Kirk would drive into the towns, walk through Main Street, greeting everyone and move on.

"I had instructed him to give no speeches and if interviewed by the press, to make no statement or answer," Lee said. "This is a tough assignment for a candidate to follow, especially with the press hammering on him to state his position on many issues. Claude did a great job until finally in one desperate outburst he answered the press by saying 'I'll answer all those questions when I release my white papers.'"

There were no white papers. But Lee contracted with a political writer to produce white papers on six issues: senior citizens, state finances, taxes, education, highways and crime. Lee wanted volume.

"I told him I wanted it measured by the inch and weighed in by the pound," Lee recounted. It took several weeks and the press continued to ask about the white papers, but they were finally finished and printed.

Kirk wanted to release them one at a time and have a press conference about each. Instead, a major press conference was called and the total package was given to the reporters who were told to call if they had questions. A newspaper man complained that it was too much to read all at once, which was Lee's strategy. From then on, whenever someone asked Kirk a question on an issue, he would respond by saying that it was complicated, but fully explained in the white papers. He continued to campaign on one thing, his opponent's liberalism.

BEARDING THE LION IN HIS DEN

Florida's incumbent Governor, Hayden Burns, had not survived a 3-way primary contest where he had been challenged by Scott Kelly, a State Senator from Lakeland and Robert King High, the Mayor of Miami. Kelly was eliminated in the first go round and High was victorious in the primary against Burns. Bob Lee, knowing Governor Burns was angry about being challenged and eliminated from another term by his own party, decided to visit the Governor and seek his support. Later, Lee wrote: "I flew up to Tallahassee, walked in the Governor's office and introduced myself to his secretary. You would have thought I was his long lost mother. He graciously invited me in and we visited for almost two hours. I told him that I knew a man of his high integrity couldn't help but be resentful by the type of campaign Mayor High had waged against him. After agreeing with this, he finally asked what he could do and then we got down to basics. He began calling some of his more powerful supporters around the state and put me in touch with them. All during the campaign I kept in continuous contact with the Governor and he was quoted on election night as saying 'how sweet it is.'"

Kirk entered the final week of the campaign as a definite underdog. Papers throughout the state were predicting a landslide victory by High, but it was not to be. Kirk, in what was proclaimed as the biggest political upset in Florida's history, not only won but did so by a landslide – by 152,957 votes – 821,194 for Kirk and 668,233 for High.

Following the election, on November 27, 1966, the "Florida Magazine" section of the Orlando Sentinel carried a major story about the election with Lee's picture on the front of the magazine. It was headlined "HOW TO BE A SUCCESSFUL REPUBLICAN BY REALLY TRYING" and started with the following quote:

" 'I thought they were smoking opium,' " is the way Robert E. Lee recalls his invitation to run the Claude Kirk campaign for governor of Florida. 'I told them no man in the United States could do the job of electing a Republican governor down there.' That was last March and eight months later Bob Lee, the organizational wizard who probably did more than anyone else to create our political revolution, is loath to take credit for the win."

In the article Lee gave all the credit for the win to volunteers. " 'I could have walked out of the state six weeks before the election and the result would have been the same' ", he said. " 'They worked around the clock, they went without meals, they spent their own money and they didn't want anything when it was over.' "

Governor Claude Kirk

After 93 Years
A GOP Governor
For Florida

Cartoon in the same article on Lee

Lee stayed on in Florida, advising the Governor-elect on appointments. The Florida Republican hierarchy as well as many of the precinct workers staged a celebration dinner at a Fort Lauderdale hotel in December commemorating the victory and honoring Kirk and Lee.

Eddie Nicholson called several of Bob's close friends in Denver and invited them to the dinner. One of these friends, Rendle Myer, recalls: "Eddie called Ralph Clark and asked Ralph, Willard Ball and me to fly to Florida to attend this dinner. We flew to Miami and were met there by a limousine which took us to a lovely home on the island waterway in Fort Lauderdale where we spent the night. That home was next to the one owned by Leonard Hall (former chairman of the Republican National Committee) where Eddie and Mary Nicholson were staying. We were asked not to see Bob until the dinner Saturday so that he would be surprised."

At the dinner Bob was delighted to see his Denver friends. The ballroom was packed with Republicans who were county chairmen and vice chairmen, precinct chairmen, block workers, campaign donors and fund raisers.

81

Myer continued: "After dinner the program started with the Republican State Chairman and the Republican National Committeeman and Committeewoman telling how Claude Kirk would not have been elected Governor of Florida without Bob Lee. Leonard Hall spoke warmly of Bob and emphasized how important Bob's political successes in Florida, New Jersey and Colorado had been to the Republican Party.

"The main speaker was Governor-Elect Kirk who thanked the Republican Party and all the workers but made it very clear that it was Bob's organizational and leadership ability that was responsible for his election. At the end of his speech, in a sincere emotional tribute to Bob, Kirk gave his Marine Corps Officer sword to Bob and they embraced. Everyone in the ballroom rose and gave Bob and Claude Kirk a rousing standing ovation that lasted several minutes. Bob then spoke briefly, thanked all who had worked on the campaign and encouraged them to stay active in the party and espouse the conservative beliefs and the goals that he believed in."

After the Ball, the Colorado contingent met at Leonard Hall's house where there was a great deal of political conversation, especially about the resurgence of Richard Nixon. Nixon's name also was mentioned in the Orlando news magazine article where the writer noted, "National attention is on Lee (this interview was interrupted by a 10-minute telephone conversation with Dick Nixon)."

Nixon, throughout his turbulent political career, was Bob Lee's hero.

Chapter 9

Bob & Bee – 1968

RICHARD NIXON –
LEE'S ROLE MODEL

Richard Milhous Nixon, the 37th President of the United States, a rough-and-tumble no-holds barred politician, was the prototype of what conservative Republicanism was all about – at least to Robert E. Lee.

Following the successful Kirk campaign in Florida, Bob did a great deal of enforced quiet thinking and reminiscing. While he, his wife, Bee, and daughter, Delisa, were staying overnight in an Orlando motel on their way back to Denver, Lee suffered a heart attack. He was taken to the Florida Sanitarium Hospital in Winter Park where he spent almost two weeks. Bee described the heart attack to inquiring reporters as "a very mild coronary – his first." Bee and Delisa had moved to Florida in May to be with Bob during the final stages of the campaign. His son, Denny, was also with him for most of Bob's seven-month stay. Eric, the Lee's oldest son, had joined the family to help move possessions, which included Delisa's horse, back to Denver.

A Denver Post story by political reporter Tom Gavin noted that Lee had gained an "almost overnight reputation as a political professional, able to work GOP organizational miracles in vast reaches where Republicans feared to tread. There's speculation, too, that the transplanted Denverite is on the verge of blossoming out as some sort of Deep South campaign strategist for former Vice President Richard Nixon, who would like another try for the presidency next year. Lee just sort of smiles when asked about the rumors."

Lee did more than smile. He obviously did a lot of thinking about Nixon and what the future held for this man that he so admired. Lee wrote from his hospital room: "My first real awareness of Richard Nixon was in his U.S. Senate race in 1950.

"Bee and I were vacationing in California and spent a day with an old college friend of mine who was in the telephone union out there. We finally worked our way around to politics. The argument became heated and I finally put a quart of whiskey on Nixon against Helen Douglas (in the race for U.S. Senate).

"The next special interest I took was in the 1952 campaign. The 'Checkers' incident created a lot of panic and many in the Party felt Nixon should resign from the ticket. My good friend, Eddie Nicholson, a close personal friend of General Eisenhower, was just as determined he should not. I listened to a lot of maneuvering.

"Then again in the pre-Convention period of 1956, I observed with interest the jockeying by some of the hierarchy of the Party to displace the then Vice President Nixon on the ticket. Again I watched Eddie Nicholson go to work and I credit Len Hall with abruptly shutting off this movement with the sharp statement about both the President's health and ability to run and that Nixon would again be the Vice President."

Lee also recalled his first meetings with Nixon which have been described in Chapter 5.

Nixon carried Colorado in 1960 by a majority of 90,000 votes even though John Kennedy won the presidency.

Lee continues his reminiscing: "By then, 1960, the Republican Party of Colorado was being rebuilt and rejuvenated. We had to take on Democrat incumbents in the U. S. Senate and the Governor's office in 1962. We needed something to kick it off. In the spring of 1961 I wanted to hold a big rally both for enthusiasm and money, providing I could get just the right person for the drawing card. Again I appealed to Nixon. We had our rally in the Denver University

Field House and sold tickets at $10 for a hot supper. They still talk about that in Denver. We jammed the place and netted over $50,000. We felt the ball was now rolling and again I owed my gratitude to Mr. Nixon."

While working the Sarcone campaign in New Jersey, Lee continued to talk frequently with Nixon. "I talked to him on several occasions in regard to our campaign," Lee later remembered. "I felt that he was genuinely interested in the results as it might be a proving ground as to what the Republican Party could do in a large industrial Eastern state.

"During the last week in October, he called me to invite me to his apartment. We spent the entire evening discussing the next year's presidential campaign. He asked me my opinion and I told him that I felt that at long last the conservatives were going to have their chance and that Goldwater would take the Convention and that he would beat Kennedy in the November 1964 election."

Lee, in his comments, said parenthetically that this prediction was based on his feelings that the Kennedy administration had alienated the Italian vote because of the Valachi expose and the entire South because of Bobby Kennedy's actions as Attorney General. "I'll never forget his answer," Bob said later. "'I think you are probably right but I've learned that just when you think something in politics is all set, something can come along to upset the entire apple cart.' It turned out to be quite a prophecy. In less than 30 days President Kennedy was assassinated and politically that bullet went right through Goldwater."

After returning to Colorado following the New Jersey campaign and being reelected Denver County Chairman, Bob immediately went to work for Goldwater.

"I had several contacts with Mr. Nixon during 1964," he said. "At the San Francisco Convention he asked me to come to his hotel suite and we spent an hour talking about the future of the Republican Party. Although it wasn't mentioned, I think both of us felt we were fighting a losing battle due to the turn of events.

"Toward the end of the campaign he called to ask what he could do for us in Colorado." Nixon had agreed to come to Colorado for a big rally and "it was all planned out when I received a call from

Nixon saying he would have to cancel because President Hoover had died and he had been asked to be a pallbearer," Lee said. The event was cancelled.

Shortly thereafter, Lee remembered Nixon again called to say he was coming through Denver on the Saturday before the election and if we wanted to put something together for that morning he was available.

"I felt that nothing was going to save the election so I decided to start right then for the future," Lee said. "We had a Saturday morning get together for our 900 precinct committeemen and women. We made this an appreciation day for a great bunch of little people who had done such a great job for the past five years. Nixon was terrific and they loved him from the start. No so-called big shots were there. They (the workers) showed their appreciation at the 1968 convention when they went all out for Nixon delegates.

"I rode out to the airport with him and he asked me to come aboard his plane and asked his staff to leave us alone for awhile. He told me that the Republicans were going to lose the election and badly. He was concerned that the liberal part of the Republican Party would use this as an excuse and attempt to take over the Party from the conservatives. Nelson Rockefeller was the leader of one faction while Nixon was the conservative champion.

"From that point on (after the Goldwater defeat) it was a case of putting the pieces back together and getting the Party morale back together where we could win some Congressional elections in 1966," Lee recalled. "In late 1965 Mr. Nixon was the principal speaker at a Denver rally. He asked me to come up to his hotel room afterwards and to bring along anyone I thought appropriate. I took along three chairmen from the large suburban counties around Denver. We spent the rest of the evening discussing the Congressional races we had a chance to win provided he (Nixon) put in some personal effort.

"I knew then that he had made up his mind to use the 1966 Congressional campaign as his base for the presidential nomination in 1968. He was willing to gamble his future and the results were outstanding, particularly when no one else, including the National Committee, put forth an all out effort."

86

Lee later admitted that his conversations with Nixon were also a factor in his agreement to go to Florida to manage Kirk's campaign. He believed that conservative Democrats in the South, which had been consistently voting Democratic since the Civil War, were closer philosophically to the Republican Party then to the Democratic Party.

After returning to Denver following his hospital stay in Florida, Bob reestablished his real estate business. But he continued to think and strategize politics – particularly Nixon for President politics. Nixon urged him to jot down his thoughts on how the Nixon campaign in 1968 should be strategized.

Lee outlined what he thought the campaign should do in three pages in very simple terms as follows:

1. Appointment of campaign chairman (Henry Bellman, Bud Wilkenson, etc.) An immediate meeting should be held to lay out the mechanics of the operation. An executive director should be appointed to assist the chairman. This person should be a thorough detail man.

2. Campaign should be divided into three separate divisions, each with their own responsibilities and reporting directly to the chairman.

   A. Convention Delegate Division. A man should be appointed chairman of this division who understands the mechanics of how to nail down committee delegates state by state. An immediate inventory of each state should be made. A file should be available as to how each state selects their delegates – who is apt to have control of these elections and who are they lining up with now. I believe it is imperative to set up a nucleus of delegates so that we have a base of operations. The delegate chairman should make a careful study and appoint area chairmen who will work five or six states for delegates. If possible, these area men should be someone who can at least control the delegates in his own state. (We are talking about a Peter O'Donnell, Bo Calloway, John Wold type.) When these men are selected, call a meeting with them, including yourself, the campaign chairman and the delegate

87

chairman. Then a complete and hardnosed analysis can be made of each state's status. If all this is done you already have committed delegate strength gathered in the room and when they go out into the field they lend an impetus to the campaign plus a real winner's image. In each state there is generally some person or persons who pretty well engineers the selection of delegates and control those delegates. It may be a governor, a senator, congressman, the state chairman or someone behind the scene. It may be that a state is divided in its control and it will have two or more factions in the delegation. These facts must be determined accurately. Once they are determined and we feel we have the power with us, then I think it is necessary for you to make a phone call and cement the commitment. No one else really can.

B. A Primary States Division. A chairman for this division should be appointed. His job is to take an inventory of all states having presidential primaries and in what states are the elected delegates committed or pledged. He should then be directed by the campaign chairman as to what states you will be a candidate. Once that decision has been made it is his job to see that a Nixon campaign chairman is appointed in each primary state and an effective campaign is planned. He should be under the direct authority of the campaign chairman.

C. A General Campaign Director. This person's entire energies should be pointed towards the November election *after the nomination*. He then should be making plans as if the nomination were already won without interfering with the pre-convention drive.

3. After this much has been started then it is time to go into much more detail. A public relations program can be started, a national finance chairman appointed with a budget worked out, scheduling, etc.

This has been over-simplified but too many campaigns are over complicated and therefore neglect the few key essentials.

I believe it is imperative to get the kind of people representing you in the field that (a) control votes and (b) give a winning new image. I know you feel comfortable with your present group and they are extremely loyal to you. If they can be used as your confidential 'Kitchen Cabinet' for advice on setting all this up, and on strategy and put the new group out as your salesman, it will be the effect needed.

Anyone can draw a beautiful set of plans on how to win an election but the really important thing is the right person selected to implement these plans. <u>PEOPLE ARE THE KEY.</u>

Lee did more than strategize. He was available to go anywhere and do anything for Nixon.

He returned to Florida in September of 1967 as the guest speaker for an event held to salute all Republican Legislators. At the head table was another special guest, Miss Susan Hayward, who presented a special plaque to each Legislator from the Executive Committee for their service to Florida and the Republican Party.

THE FLORIDA REPUBLICAN CHALLENGER

Volume 1 — THE ORIGINAL PUBLICATION OF THE FLORIDA REPUBLICAN PARTY — Number 4

ROBERT E. LEE & SUSAN HAYWARD SPECIAL GUESTS
300 GOP LEADERS AT ANNUAL MEETING

The stage is set for the all-important State Executive Annual Meeting when key Republican leaders from all over Florida will gather to exchange ideas and map strategy for 1968.

Activities scheduled will include various meetings Friday evening Sept. 15 of the State Finance Committee headed by A. Gray Boylston; elected officials committee, Chairman Charles Bolley; Senior Citizens, Dick Richards, Chairman; and Research, Research Director George Shaffer. Later that evening will be the quarterly meeting of the Executive Board.

Saturday, in addition to the Annual Meeting of the Committee various Seminar-type

presentations will be offered by our Committee Chairmen.

Legislators To Be Honored.

A gala dinner will be held saluting all Republican Legislators. Guest speaker will be Robert E. Lee, former Kirk-for-Governor Campaign Manager. Another special guest, the lovely Miss Susan Hayward will present a special plaque to each Legislator from the State Executive Committee with appreciation for their fine service to Florida and the Republican Party.

Sunday morning the political candidates will conclude with additional Seminar presentations. Over 300 Republican leaders are expected at the Thunderbird Motel in Jacksonville.

ROBERT E. LEE

SUSAN HAYWARD   Photographs by George Skadding

In 1968 Lee returned to New Jersey to help lay the groundwork to win delegates for Nixon. He travelled to Alaska to do the same. Son Eric was teaching school in Anchorage and was Alaska's Nixon chairman. Nixon had chosen Spiro Agnew of Maryland to run on his ticket as Vice President, making one of Lee's Florida political buddies unhappy.

"I wanted to be Nixon's Vice President," Governor Claude Kirk later related. "I told Bob that he should try to get me in contact with the real leaders of the Party who all would be coming to Miami and my state for the National Convention which was an acknowledgement of my victory in 1966.

"Bob said he would and he did. Besides meeting with Nixon himself, I had gotten the ear of Senator Everett Dirkson and he was big in the Party. But his son-in-law, Senator Howard Baker, was obviously his first choice.

"But I believe I was the second choice, at least he told me so. But Nixon ended up wanting Governor Agnew from Maryland. I learned later that Agnew got the nod because Onassis had contributed a half million dollars to the Nixon campaign and he had a relationship with Agnew, a fellow Greek. I told Bob later that if I had known that was how it was done I would have raised a half million.

But I did spend a lot of time later with Agnew teaching him how to be a good speaker."

The team of Nixon-Agnew won the election. Bob and Bee travelled to Washington to celebrate and attended many parties, including the inaugural ball.

During the campaign, Lee was looking for someone in Colorado to head up the Nixon effort. He found his man in William Armstrong, a young, conservative State Senator.

Bob and Bee at the Inaugural Ball

90

Chapter 10

ARMSTRONG AND DANIELS – THE LEE CONNECTION

Robert E. Lee – 1973

Bill Armstrong and Bill Daniels had three things in common: the same first name, both were in media businesses and both were conservative Republicans. It was the latter quality that caused Robert E. Lee to gravitate to both men, seeking their financial and political support for the conservative philosophy he espoused and to support each of them in their political careers.

The two had opposite reactions at their initial meetings with Bob – Daniels was impressed, Armstrong was skeptical.

"I first met Bob Lee when he brought John Love to my office during Love's campaign for Governor in 1962," Daniels, a cable television mogul, wrote. "Bob had known that I was a contributor to the Republican Party. He also knew that I had virtually no knowledge of the Party's structure.

"On that day when he brought John Love to my office, he was looking for financial support and, of course, John received it from me in each of his campaigns for governor. I was impressed with Bob's low key approach to the Love campaign and in all our conversations we only talked about his candidate, not one word about himself. This was typical of Bob, as I later learned."

Armstrong, owner of several radio stations, was first elected to the State House of Representatives when he was 25 years old. He served in the State House of Representatives and the State Senate before launching the first of his three successful efforts to represent Colorado in Washington. He followed those campaigns with two successful races for the U. S. Senate and retired voluntarily after 12 years, setting his own term limits.

"I began hearing about Bob in the middle of the 1960's but when I really began to encounter him, was in 1967, when some guys came to me and wanted me to consider being the Colorado Chairman for Nixon," Armstrong recalled in an interview September 11, 1998. "That was Jack Wogan and Dwight Hamilton. Behind them and putting them up to it was Bob Lee." Armstrong recalled that in those days there were great regional leaders that, if you were running for office, even that of the Presidency, you went to see. Bob Lee was that individual in Colorado.

"I want to tell you why I was a bit apprehensive about my first visit with Bob Lee," Armstrong said. "He was by that time a controversial figure and so was Ralph (Clark, former GOP Denver county secretary). There were rumors that they had tried to have an improper influence over John Love and that somehow they were pushy. That was true. Ralph and Bob were always pushy – but for the political ideals they espoused."

But Armstrong said he felt that there was something kind of borderline – that they might want favors that really were over the line. "I always had that fear, that here were these guys who were exercising all this power and I was concerned as to how I got drawn into that orbit and I wanted to be careful." Armstrong said, "I didn't want to get into a compromising situation where I would be asked to do something against my principles. I didn't want to do anything that would be a violation of my standards or ethics.

"I was cautious because these were guys, first of all, who were twice as old as I was, who had been at this since before I was born, and who had their own password and secret handshakes and knew all the buzz words. I was a newcomer and they were powerful. I was just a new kid on the block and you hear about corrupt politicians in big city machines. So I figured I had better be careful how I handled myself."

But Armstrong quickly added, "He never asked me to do anything that was across the line. He never hinted that he wanted to do anything that was across the line. I never saw him ask anyone else to do anything across the line. Or did he do anything himself in any way that even came close to crossing the line. But because he radiated this sense of power and was surrounded by this clique of guys of whom he was the leader, I was very, very cautious."

Lee had become embroiled in Colorado politics immediately upon his return to Colorado after the Kirk campaign in Florida and after recovering from his heart attack there.

Armstrong agreed to be Nixon's Colorado campaign manager for the 1968 campaign. "The only condition I put on the deal was that I had already made plans to take Ellen (his wife) to Europe and said I could not cancel that trip," Armstrong said. "When I returned from that trip it was time to put together the State Convention delegation. Nixon had all the votes and we could have swept the convention. We could have gotten 100% of the votes for Nixon. Instead it was decided to have a unity slate so that a broader section of the Republican Party could go to the Convention. The delegation included Governor Love."

Armstrong was most impressed with Lee and Clark in 1972 when he decided to run for Congress. He had just finished his term in the State Senate and announced his candidacy in June for the November, 1972, election. "Ralph took off two months from his job and basically became full time, but the condition on which he did this was that Bob Lee would be the volunteer coordinator," Armstrong said. "The thing that I found so astounding about that first of all, here are two of the big time pols in the area, and they are taking volunteer jobs. They weren't paid to do this, and here is Bob Lee, confidant of presidents and the guy who got Claude Kirk elected, the guy who got John Love elected. Big player on the national scene, and all of a sudden, he's sitting on the desk as a volunteer coordinator for my little campaign for the U. S. House of Representatives."

Armstrong said he learned a lot from watching Bob in action. "We had a great campaign," he said. "It was exactly the way Bob was. I've never forgotten. There are very few people in politics who understand that if you want to get somebody's support, you just don't ask them for their support, you ask them to do something and report back. And you give them a specific job.

"Bob used to say we've got hundreds of jobs here that we have to get done and if we have more volunteers than jobs, there are hundreds of jobs we can create. If someone wants to do something, don't just say, support me. He said he wanted to have a specific assignment no matter how small and to report. He said he wanted them to really feel that they had a real part in the campaign."

Since he had been out of the state so much of the time, first in New Jersey, then in Florida, then traveling the country on behalf of Nixon, Lee's real estate business suffered. In 1969 he took a full time paid position with one of John King's companies. King, chairman of King Resources Company, had set up several subsidiary companies, including Imperial American Management Company. Bob was named vice president of public affairs for this firm. It gave him a firm financial base while continuing his activities on behalf of the Republican Party, with King's full support.

Things were running well for the Republican Party in Colorado. Don Brotzman had been reelected to the Congress; Peter Dominick had been reelected to the U. S. Senate, defeating Steve McNichols. Both Houses of the State Legislature were controlled by the GOP with John Bermingham, Carl Williams and Joe Shoemaker elected to the Senate from Denver and Jean Bain, Ted Bryant, Palmer Burch, Don Friedman, Carl Gustafson and Bill Griffith, all from Denver elected to serve in the House. At the Denver County organizational level, Jack Wogan, Shirley Rigg and Neil Jones had been elected chairman, vice chairman and secretary with Bill Daniels serving as treasurer.

1969 was a hectic year in Denver with feelings running high about school busing. Federal Judge William Doyle, in 1968, had ordered students in the Denver Public Schools system, almost 88,000, to be bused out of their neighborhoods to other schools to achieve integration.

Frank Southworth, Manager of Revenue in the Batterton cabinet and Jim Perrill, Denver County Judge appointed by Batterton ran for the Denver School Board on an anti-busing program. Lee

Bob and Bee with Congressman Bill Armstrong

became involved in the campaign for his two friends, urging them to keep their campaign short and concise and repeat over and over again that they were against forced busing.

The busing issue continued to divide Denver and the Federal Court order was not lifted until 1995. Meanwhile, because of forced busing and the Poundstone Amendment which prohibited Denver from annexing land from any of the surrounding suburban counties without prior voter approval from those counties, Denver school's population dropped to 68,000.

In 1970, Republican District Attorney Mike McKevitt was elected to Congress from Denver, defeating Craig Barnes, who had upset long-time Denver Congressman Byron Rogers in a primary. John Vanderhoof, a popular Western Slope representative who had served as Speaker of the House, defeated Bill Armstrong in a Republican primary for Lieutenant Governor. In that general election, John Love won his third term for Governor by defeating Mark Hogan.

U.S. Senator Bill Armstrong

While Lee continued to work for President Nixon's reelection, he was confident Nixon would have little trouble defeating the Democratic candidate, George McGovern, so he had the time to work for Armstrong in his campaign for the U. S. Congress.

He also helped Bill Daniels become the National Committeeman from Colorado. Daniels recalls, "Bob was not comfortable with our Republican National Committeeman Bob Flanigan because Flanigan felt that money was a solution to all campaigns. He had a brother who was one of the top advisors to President Nixon, Peter Flanigan.

"Knowing my previous fund raising efforts for Republican candidates, Bob approached me to run for National Committeeman whose primary job is fund raising for political candidates. In addition, it took some heat off Bob in raising funds which he did well, but disliked doing.

"Bob talked me into going into the race. It was hotly contested. Bob and I drove to every county in Colorado and in the end I was Republican National Committeeman." Daniels served on the National Committee with Bob Dole when he was chairman. George Bush also served on that National Committee.

It was during those drives around the State, that the two started talking about Love's successor as Governor, since he would be finishing his third term. (As it turned out, Love resigned as Governor to accept presidential appointment in Washington to head up the Energy Department – a move Love later admitted was a mistake. When Love resigned, Lieutenant Governor John Vanderhoof became Governor of Colorado.)

In recalling those days, Daniels said, "Bob felt that I was a proper candidate and could win the Republican nomination. I guess my ego got the best of me and I decided to run, even though the next election was better than a year away. We had to be working hard early because Bob knew we had to set up a state-wide organization."

Many years later in a personal letter to Bill Daniels, Bob Lee wrote, "That was the worst job I ever did. I didn't know how to contest a Republican incumbent and it still haunts me."

In that Republican primary in September of 1974, Vanderhoof received 94,334 votes to 61,691 for Daniels – a respectable showing.

On the Democratic side, Richard Lamm, a Denver Representative, was polling 120,452 to 84,796 for Tom Farley of Pueblo. Lamm went on to beat Governor Vanderhoof in the November election.

Vanderhoof recalls those elections. "I was never concerned about the primary," Johnny Van recalled in a telephone conversation on October 27, 1998. "That didn't hurt me in the General Election – it was the Nixon debacle." He admired Lee's talents, "even though we didn't run in the same crowd and he was opposing what I was trying to do," Vanderhoof said. "I was kind of the country boy and he was big city, but he was a man of integrity. I wish we had individuals with his talents working with us now." His forte, Vanderhoof said, "was organizational politics. We don't have that any more – now it's big money and television."

About the time Daniels was being defeated in the Primary, President Nixon was resigning from the Presidency, succeeded by Gerald Ford. That momentous change in Washington caused Lee tremendous personal distress because of his admiration for Nixon but also was to affect his personal life and that of his family.

Bob and Sherrye, his grandaughter, and Bill Daniels

Chapter 11

Robert E. Lee – 1976

WASHINGTON –
A BRIEF INTERLUDE

Newspaper article – Thursday, April 1, 1976 – Denver Post Washington Bureau.

"The appointment of Robert E. Lee, former Denver Republican County Chairman and long time political consultant, to the Foreign Claims Settlement Commission, has been confirmed by the Senate.

"Lee, listed as owner of a consultant firm in Denver, managed the campaigns of many Colorado Republican candidates including the first one of former Governor John A. Love. In the 1960's he supervised the campaigns of Governor Claude Kirk in Florida and others outside of Colorado.

"He will have a salary of $37,800 and will be one of three members of the Commission, which determines settlements made to claimants under the International Claims Act of 1949 and the War Claims Act of 1948.

"Representative Bill Armstrong, R-Colo., said he did not propose Lee for the appointment but did endorse it. Lee is 'well qualified and has a fine character,'" Armstrong said. "Former Colorado Supreme Court Justice Leonard b.d. Sutton served on the Commission as chairman in 1968-69."

Why did Bob Lee, who constantly preached the Republican gospel of reduced government and less taxes, go to Washington, D.C., the mecca of government? His wife, Bee, supplies the best answer. "Bob was a history buff all his life and this gave him the opportunity to see where so much American history was made," Bee recalls. "I think it was one of the greatest thrills of his life when he visited the Archives and saw the original Constitution of the United States."

Lee was recommended for the Commission appointment by William Tucker, Chairman of Tucker & Associates, international trade and strategic marketing consultants in Washington, D.C. and a long time friend of Bob's. "I first met Bob Lee when I was chairman of the Denver Young Republican organization and Bob was chairman of the Denver Republican organization," Tucker said. "The young Republicans in Denver and Colorado were very active and financially strong organizations at that time and had purchased equipment for the Denver Republican County organization. We had a state convention in Greeley and my friend, Jack Stiegelmeier was running against a candidate backed by Bill Funk, the state chairman at that time. I was managing Stiegelmeier's campaign when we went to the Denver County Republican headquarters and asked Bob if we could borrow some typewriters and a reproduction machine during the convention. Bob's response was, 'Hell, yes, you paid for most of it, so take whatever you need.' We took the equipment to Greeley which helped greatly in the campaign and Stiegelmeier won the chairmanship of the Colorado Young Republicans."

Tucker knew that Bob's real estate business had been neglected because of all the volunteer time he had given to the Republican Party and its various candidates so that the timing was right to propose him for a salaried position in Washington.

"A friend of mine, Peter McPherson, who was at that time Deputy Director of White House personnel and later was administrator of A.I.D. and Deputy Secretary of the Treasury Department during the Reagan administration, called me on a regular basis about openings in White House personnel," Tucker recalls. "At this point in time, Peter called me about an opening with the Foreign Claims Commission and I proposed Bob Lee for the job."

100

Tucker said Lee did an outstanding job on the Commission and was respected by everyone he came in contact with in Washington.

When asked for thoughts for the reasons why Bob was asked to join the Commission, Bee replied in her most candid way, "I think they wanted someone older, someone who wasn't looking to a permanent career in Washington and someone who did not expect a monumental salary," Bee responded. "Actually it was very good for him and for me. Our children were grown and we enjoyed our stay in Washington."

They rented an apartment in Fredricksburg – "It was very small and we refurnished it with stuff from garage sales – and it was convenient for Bob to commute to Washington. The Commission met every Wednesday and the staff laid out the agenda." Bee said, "I would go into Washington with him for those Wednesday meetings and listen to the hearings. They were fascinating."

LEE'S TRIBUTE TO EDDIE NICHOLSON

Following Nicholson's death in 1976, Bob wrote the following letter published in the Denver Post from his home in Fredricksburg, Virginia: "As the year 1976 was nearing its close, we lost one of our dearest citizens, Edward D. Nicholson, who was known affectionately everywhere as just 'Eddie'. He was a man who loved America, his native state of Colorado, and Denver. He was an example of patriotism, loyalty and integrity throughout his long life. Born in Leadville (next door to Molly Brown) during the mining boom days, he lived to see the progress that brought Colorado up to its modern day. He was a large part of this growth. Always a sports enthusiast, he, along with Mayor Will Nicholson, brought organized baseball to Denver after World War II and also its first professional hockey team. A firm believer in the air industry, he was always an advocate for Denver's place as a center for air travel. Anywhere he went in the United States people knew him and addressed him as 'Eddie'. He was a life long friend of President Eisenhower, and when Ike had his heart attack in 1955, Eddie's house was used as the White House for those six weeks. The reason I am writing this letter now is in the hopes that (1) someone with ability

will write a complete story on his life and contributions,
and (2) that the powers that be at either the city or state
level will find a way to permanently honor this great cit-
izen. There will never be another 'Eddie Nicholson.' "

The Foreign Claims Settlement Commission was established in 1954 by merging the International Claims Commission, a unit in the Department of State, and the War Claims Commission, an agency whose sole function had been to consider war related claims. As an independent agency it acted upon the claims of United States citizens whose property abroad had been taken by foreign governments. American citizens who had suffered such losses were entitled to have their claims adjudicated without the influence of foreign policy considerations.

In one of its annual reports to the Congress, the Commission outlined its responsibilities: "The complexity of many claims, the vagueness of international law, and the interrelation of various bodies of foreign law required special legal and factual expertise. Perhaps most important, due to the deep emotional feelings many Americans felt over their losses, it was clear that only a small independent agency, whose sole function was to consider claims, could provide the personalized, efficient and responsive service often lacking when a citizen seeks relief from a massive agency of government."

During its existence the Commission handled over a million claims and made awards of several billion dollars. Funds for payment of claims came from three sources: Congressional authorizations in some of the prisoner of war internee claims programs; international claims agreements providing lump sum payments; and assets of foreign governments, blocked in this country and liquidated to pay the claims. The expenses of the Commission generally came from the same sources, so in reality, Bob's service to the Commission was not at taxpayer's expense – fulfilling his life long commitment to "lower taxes and less government."

Even so, Bee recalls, Bob was scandalized by what he considered a waste of taxpayer's money. "I remember once when he came home and ranted and raved about how all the Commissioners' offices had been refurbished and repainted," Bee said. "Gobs of

Wilford Smith, Commissioner   Raymong Beel, Chairman   Bob Lee, Commissioner

Foreign Claims Settlement Commission

money had been spent and he thought it was the most stupid thing he had ever witnessed. It just blew his mind."

Bee recalls she and Bob had the opportunity to do a lot of sight-seeing, including many visits to the Smithsonian Museums. "But probably the highlight of our stay was on the very first Christmas we spent at Williamsburg," she said. "It was wonderful – all the candle-light parades at night, midnight church services, everyone in histor-ical garb – we felt like we were back in the time of the founding fathers."

They became members of the Fredricksburg Country Club and were able to continue playing golf and tennis and, in addition, Bee remembered "we joined a duplicate bridge club." They knew their stay in Washington was temporary, however, and both were anxious to return to Colorado. The opportunity came in 1978 when Bill Daniels offered him a position in his cable television firm. Bob resigned from the Commission and returned to Colorado to start a new career with his political colleague and friend, Bill Daniels.

Chapter 12

Robert E. Lee – 1981

DANIELS, LEE – AND REAPPORTIONMENT

Bob Lee and Bill Daniels. They worked together in politics, starting with John Love's first, and successful, campaign to be Governor of Colorado and they became close friends, a friendship that lasted until Bob's death in 1998. They admired each other and enjoyed each other's company.

Bob returned to Denver to become Vice President of Daniels & Associates and spearheaded the firm's campaign to win cable television franchises in Denver and other Colorado cities. Bob strategized successful campaigns in Arvada, Aurora, Greeley and Denver.

In a letter to Bill Daniels dated March 15, 1995, Bob mentioned what great fun it was even though "I went to enough council meetings to last a lifetime." Bob, who was 81 at the time and retiring from the company, wrote a 5-page letter to Daniels "because I want you to know about my life. It's been a good life by my standards." It was in this letter that he confessed to the one real disappointment in his life – the 1974 election in which Daniels, with Lee running his campaign, lost a primary contest to the incumbent, John Vanderhoof.

He summed up his admiration for Bill Daniels as follows: "This is the hard part for me. It is impossible to say everything I think about you. I'll sum it up by saying I've never known anyone that I respect or admire more than you. What you have accomplished in so many fields is almost like reading a fairy tale. I've read many articles about you that covered many parts of your life and career but I still feel that I don't know it all and never will. I wish I knew more of your war experiences. The real story of Bill Daniels is your treatment of people. Many of the rich entrepreneurs grow into arrogant profiles. You never have. You have been the most caring person I've ever known. You have helped the unfortunate time and time again, and most of what you've done is never known by anyone else. Your employees are the luckiest people in any company anywhere. You have always taken a personal interest in their lives. You know their families, stand ready to help them when they need it. Oh, how fortunate all of us have been. You have taught us all how to treat each other with respect."

Daniels, when asked for his memories of Bob, responded with a four page letter. "Bob Lee never once asked me to do anything the entire time he was associated with me other than as a campaign manager," Daniels said. "He lived a simple life with his family and his many friends. In our shop all the secretaries loved Bob and all the guys respected him. We fell in love with his dedication to the Republican Party and as a human being. I found Bob to be humble. He walked in my office one day and said, 'How do I look?' I replied, 'Great.' He said, 'Do you notice anything different?' I replied, 'No.' He said he had just bought a new suit – the first one in 11 years. Bobby was not a clothes horse unless he was attending a function. He once told me he did not have to be well dressed when he spent most of his time, day and night, on the telephone. I do not remember him ever swearing, taking a drink, raising his voice – with the exception of a ball game or coaching Little League. Over all of his marvelous campaign contributions work and his work with the Republican Party, his favorite subject was talking about his Denver district captains."

Lessons Bob learned in working with "his Denver district captains" served him well in all the campaigns he managed, his work with the Foreign Claims Commission in Washington and, chairing a Commission charged with developing a plan to reapportion state senate and representative districts in Colorado.

Bill Daniels

Captains of political districts are responsible for finding and training precinct committeemen and women, increasing voter registration, fund raising, recruiting block workers and many other duties. It is a non-paid position but powerful and prestigious in the party structure. So Bob learned early on how to supplement efforts of captains with additional workers and assistants in a non-threatening manner, always giving captains credit for victories and downplaying his own role.

In 1981 with Daniels' full support, Lee accepted an appointment by the Chief Justice of the Colorado Supreme Court to serve as Chairman of the Colorado Reapportionment Commission. The Commission was appointed in July of 1981 to prepare a plan for reapportionment of the state senatorial and state representative districts. The Commission had the responsibility of reapportioning the districts based on the 1980 census, as mandated in a constitutional amendment adopted by the voters of Colorado.

The apportionment had to be accomplished under the following guidelines:

1. The population of legislative districts for respective houses of the general assembly must be as nearly equal as may be, but in no event may there be more than a 5% deviation between the most populous and least populous districts;
2. Each district is to be as compact in area as possible and the aggregate linear distance of all district boundaries shall be as short as possible;
3. Counties may be split into more than one district only when necessary to achieve equal population among the districts;
4. The number of municipalities with territory contained in more than one district must be as few as possible;
5. Communities of interest (ethnic, cultural, economic, trade area, geographic and demographic) are to be preserved within a single district whenever possible.

All cities and counties, both major political parties, and, especially, the 35 elected state senators and 65 elected state representatives watched with a great deal of interest and some apprehension as the Commission started its work. In previous years, before the

Commission was created, the Legislature itself was charged with reapportionment but the process was highly politicized.

In an effort to "depoliticize" the reapportionment process, Commission members had to be appointed as follows: One by the Speaker of the House (Representative Carl B. Bledsoe); one by the Minority Leader of the House (the late Representative Richard Castro); one by the Majority Leader of the Senate (Senator Cliff Dodge); one by the Minority Leader of the Senate (current Mayor of Denver, Wellington Webb); three by the Governor (Carol Edmunds, Senator Ron Stewart, and Representative Reuben Valdez); and four, including the Chairman, by the Chief Justice of the Colorado Supreme Court (Polly Coleman, Jeannie Jolly, Benjamin Loye, and Bob Lee.)

Republicans gained a six to five majority on the Commission because Paul W. Hodges, who was Chief Justice of the Supreme Court, was, according to a Denver Post editorial of March 8, 1982 "an old GOP stalwart." He had been expected to name at least one respected neutral to the body, but instead, again according to the Denver Post "he packed it with four Republican wheel horses." Nonetheless, under Lee's leadership, the 11-member Commission, after holding a series of meetings throughout the state, presented a reapportionment plan that was adopted unanimously by both the House and the Senate.

The Colorado Supreme Court upheld the plan except one small portion which would have given a district in Denver two senators for two years, while a new district had none for that time. That problem was resolved.

Reuben Valdez, appointed by the Democratic Governor from the House of Representatives, had nothing but praise for the work of Lee as Chairman.

"Bob did a superb and fair job," Valdez said. "He didn't flout his chairmanship at all. All his meetings were open. He established several sub-committees which held meetings throughout the state. He shared power with the sub-committees. For instance, I chaired Commission meetings in the San Luis Valley and Pueblo." Valdez recalled driving literally hundreds of miles throughout Colorado with Bob. They talked sports as well as politics. "We became friends, and remained friends," Valdez recalled.

109

Mayor Webb concurred. He said he enjoyed his work with Bob and the Commission and particularly enjoyed seeing political pros like Bob Lee and Bev Bledsoe at work. "Wilma (Mrs. Webb) and I valued Bob's friendship and we appreciated his kindness and forthright manner," the Mayor said.

Leonard Campbell, one of two attorneys who represented the Commission before the Supreme Court, also praised Lee's skills in directing the work of the Commission. "Even though the Republicans controlled the Commission, Bob never abused that political power," Campbell said. "Even on the appeal to the Supreme Court, he made sure that the two appointed attorneys were from differing political parties." (Campbell is a Democrat and the other attorney was a Republican, Jon L. Holm.)

Carol Edmunds Sullivan, another appointee of the Governor, complimented Bob after the Commission's work was accomplished. "Thanks largely to your sensitivity, we were able to carve out a plan rather than to snipe at each other in the midst of a stalemate," she said. "If you ever lead any political race in Colorado, I'm betting on your candidate – your political radar is unsurpassed. I was also impressed by your gracious manner with the public, whenever anyone, whatever his political persuasion, testified before us."

Lyle Kyle, who was director of the Legislative Council at the time remembered that Lee was very suspicious of the Legislative Council and its staff because the Council had done the bulk of the work for the Legislature in the 1960 and 1970 reapportionment efforts. "He insisted that the offices be away from the capitol," Kyle said. "I urged him to use David F. Morrisey as staff director for the study, which he eventually did." Morrisey, Kyle said, had been the key legislative staff member in previous reapportionment work. In an interview with the Colorado Statesman on November 20, 1981, Lee praised Morrisey and the Legislative Council staff that worked with him.

"The size of the staff totals eight," Lee said, "These people know exactly what they are doing. They are dedicated, non-partisan and they've just been excellent. We got them on loan from the Legislative Council and they will be back to the Council later."

The original appropriation by the Legislature for the reapportionment was $500,000 which included all travel costs and the costs of the salaries of the Council members while they were on loan to the Commission.

THE GOLDEN SCREW OR GILDED THREAD AWARD

This "award" was given to the Reapportionment Commission in 1982 by Dan Campbell, news editor of the Estes Park Trail-Gazette. He created this award "to be mailed out to persons and organizations whose actions do the most to reverse the fortunes of our mountain community." It was sent to Cliff Dodge, State Senator and Commission member because Senator Dodge made the motion to place Estes Park into a new senate district comprised mostly of Western Slope counties. The "award" letter stated: "Dear Cliff, Congratulations! Because of fine work the Colorado Reapportionment Commission did in responding to the testimony of the citizens of Estes Park regarding our state senate district situation, we have bestowed the coveted Golden Screw award on the Commission. Since it was your proposal to place western Larimer County in a West Slope senate district, you were singled out for the honor, but please share it with all the other members who voted for your plan. If you'd like to send us your acceptance speech or any other remarks, we'd be glad to print them. Sincerely, Dan Campbell."

The Commission completed its work on March 15, 1982, meeting all deadlines established by legislation and finished its work within budget.

After completing that task, Lee used his legislative and lobbying skills to assist the National Cable Television Association in gaining Congressional approval of what was known as the "Cable Bill." The officers of the Association sent a letter to Bob on October 24, 1984, thanking him for his efforts. "Because of you and the hundreds of other members of the cable industry who pitched in time and time again, Congress got cable's message," the letter stated. "Today cable is taking its rightful place in our nation's communication policy alongside broadcast and telephone. This is truly an historic event of enormous significance. Quite simply, it couldn't have been done without you."

As was his custom when in Washington, D.C., Bob would make courtesy calls to members of Congress. One day he and Bill Daniels dropped in to the office of Senator Nancy Kassabaum (R.Kan.) unannounced and asked to see the Senator. Her secretary told him that was impossible – she was in a meeting and could not be disturbed. "It's important," Bob said. "Please give her this note." The secretary did – and Senator Kassabaum immediately left the meeting, rushed to the outer office and threw her arms around Bob.

A perplexed Daniels later asked Bob what was in the note. The note stated, "I understand that you are as beautiful now as when I last held you in my arms." As a young man in Topeka, Bob had dated a close friend of Governor Alf Landon's (later GOP presidential candidate) daughter. Alf was at the time married to his second wife, Senator Kassabaum's mother, and Bob often held Nancy as a baby while visiting the Landon home.

Lee and Daniels continued to be the closest of friends. Daniels recalls what he termed "one of the saddest but at the same time one of the loveliest experiences of my life." It was in March of 1996, he said, when he became quite ill and was unable to travel. "It wasn't until 1997 that I was able to make a few trips to Denver from my California home close to Eisenhower Medical Center," Daniels said. "Finally the doctors put a no travel restriction on me for about six months before Bob died. Bob had not seen me in about a year. He called me one day and said that he would like to come to California and spend some time with me. At that time I knew of his health problems and was in weekly contact with Bee and others about his physical ailments.

"To put it simply, Bob knew he was dying. I flew Bob from Denver in my airplane and had James, my houseman at Cableland, accompany him on the trip. James rented a convertible, put the top down and Bobby wore a cap suitable for California convertible driving and I was waiting in front of my home when they drove up. Bob did not feel well, coughing badly, but we talked for about three hours. I then had James take him to the hotel and have him get some rest. We said goodby the next morning. Bobby and I both knew that

Bob and James Riede arriving at Bill's home

we would never see each other again. Not a word was said, but we both knew it. He cried as he left, and so did I. His death brought an end to a lovely relationship. While my doctors would still not let me travel to the funeral, I spent the entire day in my home with the lights out, talking to no one, in memory of Bob. I still think of him every day."

To that beautiful thought, Robert E. Lee's family and friends add a heartfelt "Amen."

Chapter 13

Robert E. Lee – 1996

LEE'S
LATER YEARS

On June 24, 1996, at the Annual Lincoln Day Dinner at the Denver Athletic Club, Bob Lee was given the Paul Swalm Denver Republican Lifetime Achievement Award.

Attached to the program was a short biography of Bob's life – his college life, his move to Denver, military service, real estate business and his political career. It noted that Bob and Bee had just celebrated their 57th wedding anniversary, that they had three children, five grandchildren and two great-grandchildren.

The last paragraph of this tribute to Bob Lee states: "Bob recently retired from Daniels & Associates. He remains active in Republican politics and continues to be sought out for advice and guidance by candidates for offices from city council to the Presidency of the United States."

Former U.S. Senator Bill Armstrong recalls how Bob always was available to give advice and counsel. "I don't remember what year it was," Armstrong said, "nor do I remember the issue. But I asked him his opinion about some political issue. I remembered how he handled it. He got on the phone and made about a hundred telephone calls. He didn't just give me his gut reaction. And you know guys our age and on up tend to operate on instinct and past experience. That instinct is very good. If you have a lifetime in politics your instincts are very good. But Bob was a guy who always sought fresh data. If you asked him how the winds were blowing in the state, he would get on the phone and make a hundred telephone calls. And call you back to say, 'Here's what's going on.' He wouldn't just be giving you his interpretation of the newspaper, he would be giving you a synthesis of what he had learned from talking to people at the grass roots. I never forgot that. There are very, very few senior people, senior in position and senior in years, that retain that ability."

While he freely gave his sage political advice to Republican candidates, he rejected many offers of full time employment by successful candidates, including an offer from George Bush – later President Bush – in his bid for election to the U. S. Senate in Texas. In a letter to Bob, dated June 24, 1964, Bush said: "I am sorry that you feel that you can't come here. We need you bad and I know that you could have done the job. . . If you ever start to weaken and think you can come, please don't hesitate to call." In his concluding paragraph, Bush again urged Bob to accept his offer: "I wish there was some way I could talk you into reconsidering, but in any event I am grateful to you for your hours of listening and helping out with the problems." Bob, on the letter, noted in his own handwriting that "I couldn't do this because of my commitments to the Goldwater campaign."

Perhaps Bob was emulating one of his heros, General Robert E. Lee, whose sense of loyalty caused him to reject many lucrative job offers. While he was President of Washington College after the Civil War, General Lee, in 1868, was offered the opportunity to head a large firm to represent Southern Commerce. Even though a large sum of money was placed at his disposal, he declined and wrote: "I am grateful, but I have a self imposed task which I must accomplish – to train young men to do their duty in life." (*From Lee: The Last Years*, by Charles Bracelen Flood.)

In another hand written note on his own stationery, Bob commented on other offers as follows: "Congressman William Armstrong asked me to go to Washington as his Chief of Staff. He finally got (Howard) Probst. Dick Johnson (20 years as Director for the Republican Senate Election Committee) wanted me to be his deputy. I declined. Postmaster Summerfield, former State Chairman of Michigan, (touted as the biggest Chevy dealer in the U. S.) came down to Fort Lauderdale to talk me into being the Manager of a U.S. Senator's campaign – "big bucks." Rendle Myer called one evening and said that Federal District Judge Fred Winner was going to appoint me trustee of a huge bankruptcy case. Rendle said it would probably be $100,000 for some years and I thought all night because I knew I would have to dump Bill Daniels' race for governor and I couldn't do that. I called Rendle early in the morning, thanked him and told him I couldn't do it."

In this same memorandum, he also detailed attempts to buy his influence with candidates, including one from an individual Bob referred to as "the big banana of the Bahamas." He also recounted an offer of $50,000 to "gather the Republican organization together" to support a particular candidate who was not a Republican.

His personal disclosure of refusing to accept this kind of money for services rendered does not come as a surprise to anyone who knew Bob Lee, whose honesty and integrity in the political process was admired by members of both parties.

His disdain for money that contaminated the political process was highlighted in an interview in the June 28, 1996 Colorado Statesman. This article by Roy Mall is reprinted here not only to show this disdain but also his continuing commitment to his conservative philosophy:

"'We pay too much attention to money,' Lee charged about modern day politics. 'Newspapers always report how much a candidate is raising as if it is the only barometer of how a candidate is doing. I can speak to a number of campaigns where the loser had the most money,' he said. He pointed to this year's presidential hopeful Steve Forbes, U.S. Senate candidate Michael Huffington of California and Bruce Benson in the 1994 Colorado gubernatorial race as examples of too much money and not enough fundamental campaigning. . .

"A lot of people credit Lee with the political turn-around in the South, but he thinks it was the voters – traditional family-oriented conservatives – who slowly crossed the aisle on their own accord and helped build the GOP's southern state stronghold. 'The South had gradually gotten away from the Democrats,' Lee said. 'The West,

The Colorado

STATESMAN

FOUNDED IN 1898 ★ VOL. 97, NO. 26 ★
DENVER, COLORADO ★ JUNE 28, 1996 ©

Bob Lee - a true statesman

By Roy Nall

There are two things wrong with American politics: greed and money, according to 82-year-old Robert E. Lee, a longtime Republican party stalwart and former head of the Denver County Republican party. Revered these days as a true statesman, Lee guided the GOP in the capitol city from 1958 to 1966, a time many consider to be the party's golden years.

Lee was honored this week by his Denver party peers with the Paul Swalm Lifetime Achievement Award at their annual Lincoln Day dinner. Former gubernatorial hopeful Steve Schuck bestowed the award, thanking Lee for his wisdom through the years.

The audience of over 400 also included former Colorado Supreme Court Chief Justice William Erickson, a close political friend, and former Gov. John Love.

Lee is probably best known for recruiting Love to run for governor when he was just an unknown lawyer from Colorado Springs. He

Continued on Page 6

82-year-old Robert E. Lee takes a humble pose during the Denver Republican Lincoln Day Dinner where he was honored Monday

The Denver Dems' dilemma

By Roy Nall

You might call it the case of the missing paperwork, or perhaps the case of the delinquent candidate, but either way a messy chapter in Denver Democratic politics came to an end this week when a judge overruled Secretary of State Vikki Buckley's decision to keep State Sen. Doug Linkhart and State Rep. Gloria Leyba off the August primary ballot due to missing paperwork.

As an aftershock of the ruling, two-term Denver Democratic Chair Francine Miran resigned her powerful position.

The paperwork snafu was the last straw for Miran, who has taken criticism this year for several of her actions.

"I believe this decision is in the best interest of the party that I am committed to and have served for many years. The fighting which is currently happening is too destructive. I believe my decision will force everyone to concentrate on

Continued on Page 9

Legislation kicks in next week

By Scott Anderson

Come July 1, many of the fruits of the legislative session will be ripe for the picking as numerous bills become law.

The 120-day session spawned 615 bills, with more than 55 percent skating through both houses of the legislature and making it onto Gov. Roy Romer's desk.

Despite the number of bills which survived committee, floor readings and votes, Romer issued a record high 19 vetoes this year, but described the session as "satisfactory" and declined to give a letter grade as he has done previously.

But legislators from both sides of the aisle said they hope the session will be remembered for more than the Bronco stadium bill, soaring speed limits and fluttering state bugs, which have already gone into effect; or same sex-marriage debates and growing hemp, legislation which failed.

Democrats and Republicans agreed the state's $8.8 billion budget, most of which begins the first of the month, was one of the year's greatest bi-partisan achievements.

Battle ground legislation such as revisions to the Children's Code, and enterprise zone amendments also topped both party's list of pending

laws and reforms that will officially become the law of the land next week.

The Budget

Colorado's multi-billion dollar budget is easily the largest chunk of legislation that goes into effect July 1.

Uncertainty stemming from the federal government's own squabbles over a fiscal year budget seeped into Colorado's legislature before the session even got off the ground. But discussions over whether to give the states individual block grants, welfare reform and Medicaid restructuring eventually faded into the mist, allowing Colorado's legislators, some begrudgingly, to begin work on a massive budget blueprint.

Some of the highlighted changes in this year's budget include:
• Transportation: $158.5 million was transferred from the general fund to the highway fund.
• Capital Construction: $100 million for construction and maintenance of higher education, prisons and other state buildings.
• School finance: $2.9 billion for public schools with $122 million in new funding.
• Higher Education: Added funds to limit resident tuition increases to 2.3 percent; $4.5 million

increase for student aid; and $1 million salary increase for part-time community college instructors.
• Children's budgetary considerations: $11.8 million increase in child welfare services; $7 million funding for Youth

Prevention/Positive Intervention grants, community-based crime prevention programs for youth, an increase of $2 million; $1 million increase in Child Health Plan to

Continued on Page 11

A tale of Hank Brown and drugs

By Jerry Kopel

U.S. Senator Hank Brown is getting a bum rap!

The Colorado senator is attempting to repeal a loophole in the GATT trade treaty that gives brand-name drug patent holders an additional three years of unintended monopoly (from 17 years to 20 years). Some press reports infer his efforts are all because major generic drug maker Geneva Pharmaceuticals Inc., is based in Colorado.

The truth is Sen. Brown's efforts to lower costs for consumers through generic drugs goes back to 1976 when he was Senate sponsor of HB 1087, carried in the House by me and Rep. Frank Traylor. This bill allowed generic drug substitution for brand name drugs under strict equivalency

guidelines and only when not specifically prohibited by the physician.

Lobbying to kill HB 1087 in the Senate were Jon Holm for the Pharmaceutical Manufacturers Assn., and three "detail" men from Eli Lilly, Sandos and Merck, plus a hostile Health Committee chairman Ted Strickland, plus a hostile Senate President Fred Anderson, plus the Colorado Medical Association, plus Pharmacy Board Executive Secretary Fred Simmons.

On the side of the angels were lobbyist Fred Sievers for the pharmacists, Pharmacy Association Executive Director Merle Meyers, and an astute Sen. Brown who worked his way carefully around the

Continued on Page 11

Bob being interviewed by *Colorado Statesman* June 28, 1996

it is conservative as well, but the key now for Republicans is winning the South,'" he forecast.

"But Republican victories aren't as important to Lee as his concern for the future of the two party system. 'This country has been served well for more than 150 years by two parties,' he said. 'It would be unfortunate chaos if America went the way of France or Israel, where 20 or 30 parties fight it out for a majority,' he explained. 'At least the voters have a clear choice. It changes from time to time, but there is a clear choice. I have been watching what has been going on in Russia. Oh my goodness, what a mess they are having,' Lee said. He advises those in control of both major political parties to clean up their act, take greed and money out of the game and return the politics to its roots of people-to-people contact.. . . . 'I'm a great believer in a candidate walking the streets, talking to neighbors,' he said. 'I remember people coming up to me and asking, 'Why are you a Republican?' Lee recalled. 'The Democrats' penchant for taxing and spending is one significant reason. I remember a Democratic function when Bernie Hopkins got up and said, 'We will tax, we will spend and we will elect,' and I think that has been the Democratic party's creed through 60 years – to get more control of the public. I've been scared to death of total socialism in this country. I've got people saying it will never happen in America. I think it is happening every day. Since 1932, every Congress has pushed for more taxes, more spending, more control, and if that isn't socialism, I don't know what is,' Lee said."

His fear of "tax and spend" is apparent in the following short essay that, apparently, was put together for his own edification since it was not addressed to anyone:

"QUESTION: How much of your gross income is taken in taxes by politicians? In a six month period of talking with approximately 600 people the answer was 25-45%. There were a few who said taxes exceeded the 45% mark; smart people.

"EASILY IDENTIFIED TAXES: Federal Income Tax; State Income Tax; City Income Tax; Social Security Tax; Real Estate Tax; Sales Tax; The elderly are now being taxed on their Social Security income.

"SPECIAL TAXES: Medicare Tax; Gasoline Tax; Alcoholic Beverages; Tobacco Products; Alcohol and Tobacco may be very unpopular, but they put millions of dollars in the governments' pockets.

"Every time you pick up the telephone you pay a tax. Although it is very small, think of the millions of people who use the telephone and thereby put money into government coffers!

"In your home alone, taxes are paid on natural gas, electricity and cable TV.

"Each time you fly on an airplane or rent a hotel room for the night, you pay a tax.

"Many cities collect a seat tax for concerts, plays, sporting events, etc.

"If you go to a racetrack to place a bet, you pay a tax.

"If you buy a lotto ticket, you pay a tax and, if you are lucky enough to win, the government takes a hugh amount in taxes.

"There are three taxes that I've always felt were unjust:

1. The Gift Tax: A person works all of his/her life to save a little money and some amass large amounts which is taxed as it is earned. If these individuals want to share their money with friends or relatives taxes are paid on gifts of more than $10,000.00. That is double taxation!
2. Inheritance Tax: Similar to the gift tax. Again, double taxation!
3. Capital Gains Tax: This has slowed down our economy in many ways. Most countries have a very small tax or none at all. Check Japan and Germany.

"The biggest tax of all is the hidden tax that is built into the cost of every item a consumer buys. Example: If a consumer buys an automobile for $20,000.00, he/she will pay 7 1/2% sales tax. When he/she receives the title he/she has to pay an ownership tax and a license fee. Imagine how many taxes are built into the auto before it hits the dealer's showroom floor!

"I'm sure I've missed many, many taxes that are easily identified. But, to sum it up, I believe the total taxes would be far more than 45%.

"I believe, too, that if people knew what an enormous amount they were giving the politicians, they would scream their heads off.

"P.S. If people were allowed to keep more of their income, think how much it would boost our economy!"

His philosophy of precinct organization also never wavered. On April 14, 1997, Bob gave the following written advice to two candidates:

"Remember, Rome wasn't built in a day!

"There isn't any magic in politics. Just keep it simple.

"As you are building your organization, look for quality before quantity. With 50 plus precincts, you should sooner or later recruit about 10-11 area coordinators to work with 5-6 precincts. Your personal success depends upon this group. Be sure each one is a solid conservative Republican, loyal to you, and wants to do the job right.

"You can explain to the committee people that you are making this plan so they all will have good communications at all times and the coordinators are there to help them.

"Now, get together with your coordinators and explain to them that their jobs are to help the committee people and eventually they will trust them. But, along the way they should rate the committee people; good, bad, in between but with help could be good.

"After a couple of weeks, set up a meeting so you can get a report on how they are moving along. As they progress with the committee people they can show them how to build block workers (year round). The more people you give a little title to with the party, the more votes we will have.

"You should get your tools together. Maps for your entire district and the maps for each precinct. And you will need voter registration lists.

"Run your district and ignore the other districts. Show 'em how no liberals wanted!!!!

"Good luck. I know you'll do just fine!" Bob Lee

Dan Thomasson, a reporter for the Rocky Mountain News, before being made Vice President of Scripps Howard Newspapers in Washington, D.C. wrote a personal letter to Bob congratulating him on receiving the Denver Republican Lifetime Achievement Award in 1996. Dan's letter, which captures the personality and philosophy of Lee, follows: "When Will Rogers first applied for a passport, he was told he had to produce a birth certificate. 'A certificate that I was born?' Rogers said incredulously. 'Well, where I come from if folks just saw you walkin' around, they assumed you was born.' Well, that's the way most people feel about you, Bob. We've been watching you walking around achieving things for all these years so we just assume that's reward enough. But, old friend, it is nice that the Grand Old Party still has enough sense to honor someone who has done about as much to help maintain the two party system as anyone I know.

"I'm taking personal pleasure from this, Bob, because I learned more about grass roots politics from you in five years than I have in the other 32 since I left Denver (thanks to your help). I remember a good many years ago receiving a call from Jack Knight who, as you know, among other things owned the Miami Herald. He said he had been told that I was (a) good friend of yours and since you were in a campaign in Florida, he wanted to know about you.

"'Mr. Knight,' I said. 'Four things you should remember. He's tough. He's smart. He's honest and you should always put your money on his candidate.' I always relate how you told me who was going to be the vice presidential candidate in 1968 and I thought it was way off the wall. I blew the story. It was a big mistake that I never made again. Bob, thanks for all the years you've devoted to helping make this wonderful system of ours work. And thanks for being a good pal, who always had time to teach a green kid. Wish I could be there for your big night.

"All the best always, Dan K. Thomasson."

A memorial service for Robert E. Lee was held at 2:00 p.m. Thursday, July 9, 1998 at First Plymouth Congregational Church. Bob's granddaughter, Sherrye Lee drew the following picture that graces the memorial program.

IN LOVING MEMORY
OF

ROBERT E. LEE
MARCH 15, 1914 – JULY 3, 1998

Chapter 14

Bob & Justin (Delisa's son)

MEMORIES: FAMILY & FRIENDS

FAMILY

ELIZABETH BEE JOHNSTON LEE (Born in Monte Vista, Colorado, moved with her parents to Denver, when she was six; married Robert E. Lee, June 3, 1939, Independence, Missouri):

"For 59 years and one month, I was very happy to be married to a lovely and interesting man. Those of you who read this would agree. He was admired or loved or revered, or all three.

"His wonderful disposition was one of the first things that attracted him to me, as well as his tolerance and intelligence. His open, gentle personality attracted people to him. He liked everyone he met. Bob had a good image of himself and he lived up to it.

Bob and Bee

"Many people, including Bob's mother, did not think our marriage would last. His mother even tried to get the marriage annulled. On reflection, she probably thought I was too young for Bob – after all, I was just 19 when we met, and Bob was 25. Perhaps that's why the Dean of Women at Washburn College, where I was a sophomore, wrote to my parents in Denver stating that in her opinion, I should not be dating Bob Lee. Well, we didn't date too long. Just before my sophomore year ended, Bob told me we were going to get married – he didn't ask me – he just told me.

"He always loved sports and young people. That is probably why he was such a good father.

"When we first returned to Denver, Bobby was just getting started in the real estate business with my father but yet he found the time to form and coach a team in the Young America League. Baseball and football – that took a lot of time – practices every Monday, Wednesday and Friday in Washington Park. On Saturdays they had games with teams all over Denver. The only help I gave him was to support his endeavors with these little boys and always have a late dinner ready for him when he came home.

"In college when he wasn't competing, he was teaching a tennis class and he even enjoyed impromptu softball games in the park.

"He played in many local tennis tournaments in Denver and participated in American Athletic Union basketball games and tournaments.

"Even though politics kept him away from the family a great deal of the time, nonetheless he was always there when the children needed him and was an attentive father and loving husband.

"His involvement in politics gave us an opportunity to travel – to political conventions, to Florida for the Kirk campaign, to Washington, D.C. for his work with the Foreign Claims Commission. Living in Washington gave us the opportunity to see almost every memorial, statue, museum, government building and historical place in Washington and the entire area.

"He particularly enjoyed his work and friendship for and with Bill Daniels. They shared many times – both good and bad – together. They sympathized with each other during illnesses and supported each other in some of those difficult times.

"Bob lived life to the fullest and I thoroughly enjoyed an important part of it."

ERIC LEE (Bob's oldest son, born in Denver February 17, 1941):

Eric

"I remember Dad as a good father, a wonderful coach and an individual who never lost his temper. In fact, we were always kind of afraid to make Dad mad because we didn't really know what to expect if he really did get mad. Athletics was kind of the center of our entire life. I started my athletic career in the Young America League. He coached my brother, Denny, not me, but even so, he would critique the team I was playing for and would coach me at home in our "home" basketball court that he built by our house. During those coaching sessions he always stressed fundamentals. He would go over minute details, over and over and over again.

Jason and Kendall,
Eric's son and daughter

"He was always proud of our athletic successes in high school, at South High, and later, at the University of Colorado. I'm sure his early coaching and stress of fundamentals laid the groundwork for the successes we had.

"I remember Dad playing AAU basketball and how friendly and compassionate he was to all his teammates and even his opponents.

"He always shared with us his accomplishments in college. While most of his friends knew he was a great football, basketball and tennis player, few knew that he was also a

127

sprinter and held the record for the low hurdles in Kansas, a record that stood for many years.

Eric's daughter Kelly and
Bob and Bee's three great grandchildren

"We spent a lot of time together through my childhood and through my college years which ended in my graduation in 1963 from the University of Colorado.

"Even though I lived in Alaska for 16 years, we always communicated and remained close until his death. He was a good father and we were good friends."

DENNY LEE (Bob's second son, born in Denver, July 30, 1943):

"Dad always made time to be involved in all aspects of our lives. All of us, including Lisa, enjoyed athletics and other competitions. Therefore, much of Dad's time with each of us, was involved with our "sports." Many of my fondest memories are sports stories. And Dad loved to tell stories on all of us and me in particular since I was

Denny & Bob in Topeka

a good target and provided him with good comic material.

"He particularly liked to tell the story about how while he was coaching me in Young America League football when I was nine or so, our team was whistled for two penalties in succession. Dad, in frustration, yelled across the field and demanded to know who the penalty was against. The referee called back that the penalties were for lining up offside by "the kid with the silver tooth." That was me. I had lost an encounter in some fracas and broke off half a front tooth which was capped with silver.

Denny's daughter, Sherrye, and Bob

"He also liked to tell about the time he was running late for one of our South High School baseball games. Just as he parked his car behind left field, a ball came sailing over the fence and hit the car. I was the batter.

"I especially treasure the late Friday night talks Dad and I had after the end of my South High School basketball games. No matter how late I returned home, Dad would be waiting up for me and we could talk about the game and how I could improve. We loved to argue over specific plays – but he was seldom wrong in either his recollection of events or in his analysis. He once told me to forget about being a "rebounder" and concentrate on "dribbling" because I wouldn't be getting many rebounds against the "big boys" in college. He was right on about that.

"We became "pals" in Florida. I taught him golf, and he taught me tennis. We loved to get friends together and drive to Fort Lauderdale to watch the Dolphins play.

"We saw three Super Bowls together, including Vince Lombardi's last Packer game and also Super Bowl III where Joe Namath promised a win for his New York Jets over the favored Baltimore Colts.

"We also went to several college bowl games. Dad and I literally died together when our Kansas Jayhawks lost an Orange Bowl Game in 1969 to Joe Paterno's Penn State Nittany Lions. We thought we had won the game when Kansas stopped Penn State's 2-point conversion attempt. However, K.U. had 13 men on the field and Penn State succeeded on scoring on the next play.".

DELISA LEE FALSETTO (Bob's daughter, born in Denver, June 9, 1952):

Delisa

"I was my father's favorite daughter. We had a wonderful relationship. My daddy never said no to me. My mother sometimes made unhappy noises about this, but it sure made me happy.

"Mom and I didn't like politics like Dad did, but she and I sure did like the perks that came with his profession or obsession with politics.

"One year we were with Dad in New York City. The trainer of my first horse was a contestant in a famous horse show, the last show held in the old Madison Square Gardens, which we attended.

Delisa's son, Justin, age 5

"While there we met Richard Nixon and Bebe Rebozo in the lobby of our hotel. Of course, they knew Daddy, so we stopped and chatted and this was very special for me.

"Mom got to go to two Kentucky Derbies with Dad. At one of these she and Dad sat with the presenter and he put the rose blanket on the winning horse. Unfortunately, I was too young to go any place where there was betting so I didn't get to see the Derby.

"My folks enjoyed several governor's conferences held in prestigious

130

places throughout the United States. One of their favorites was when then Governor Reagan invited them to a wine tasting party hosted by Mrs. Reagan. Edith Head, the well known designer, presented a fashion show with models wearing her new creations.

"The conventions were not that exciting for me. I would rather have stayed home in Denver playing kick the can with my friends. We had 23 grade and junior high school kids in our one block on South Linden Way.

"Both my brothers loved competitive sports. I loved horses. One of the great thrills of my life was the present I received from Mom and Dad, a young colt I named Dreamer. Friends of Mom and Dad, like Martha and Jim Romer and Bud Hover let us pasture him with their horses. Susie Balenseifer was a horse trainer and taught both me and Dreamer. We entered horse shows all over Colorado. Together we won many ribbons in the jumper and hunter classes. Now my dreams continue to come

Bob with his and Bee's three granddaughters, Kelly, Kendall and Sherrye

true. I have a house I love, a flower garden, a vegetable garden, a newborn, and three horses.

HORSING AROUND

The Lee family, through several generations, had a fondness for horses. Before the turn of the century, Bob's grandfather, Reverend Phinnias Booth Lee, depended on a horse and buggy to keep in contact with his scattered congregation. Rad Lee, Bob's father, worked with horses on the farm and, as a boy, entertained dreams of being a jockey – until, literally, he outgrew that possibility. Delisa, Bob's daughter, inherited the love of horses and became an expert and avid rider.

"Justin, my 9-year old son is the joy of my life. And you might guess that the first present he received from his Grandfather Bob, was a regulation basketball and hoop."

FRIENDS

ED ALEXANDER

"Bob and Bee Lee were the "all American neighbors," fun to be around, generous by nature, with a wonderful family and more importantly a wonderful attitude about their family. At our annual block party on the 4th of July on South Linden Way, Bob provided one of the most exciting attractions for the children. Each year he arranged for riding horses which he rented from a nearby riding stable. Bob led those horses up and down the street with delighted kids riding on their backs. Bob was an unusual man. During his career he developed friendships with a variety of people with great influence in the world of the rich and famous. Yet he seemed untouched by ambition of fame or wealth and preferred to use his considerable talents behind the scenes to help elect people that he believed could improve government."

JIM ASPINWALL

"Bob knew and loved the Constitution of the United States and always seemed to have one in his pocket. He expected government leaders to adhere to the Constitution."

PETE ATKINS

"I was asked to run for Regent of C.U. by Bob. I was pretty much ignored at the State Convention as the Party had bigger fish to fry. I ended up on the bottom line and then told Bob Lee to stuff it as no one had ever won from the bottom line. He persuaded me to stay with it and said that he would work personally on my campaign. He delivered. I came off the bottom line and beat Fred Betz, Jr. in November."

HANK BROWN

"Bob's political philosophy was as straight forward as anyone I know. He simply thought that people ought to have a chance to spend their own money instead of having it taken away from them by government. Bob made a difference in this world because he cared about a philosophy and was willing to go to work to make it come to fruition. His energy, drive and organizing ability influenced all those who knew him. He helped guide Colorado politics for both his and the next generation."

TED BRYANT

"I wanted to become a candidate for the District 13 House Seat in 1964, so I went to visit Robert E. Lee. He said, 'First you visit with each Committeeman and Committeewoman and then come back to see me.' After making these visits, I went back to Bob and he told me, 'Now go see them again.' I did. Then Bob started to coach me in the art of campaigning. Bob really didn't believe in primaries, as he thought you should have done your homework before primary time. Jeannie Meyer and Tim Treece, the captains, had a straw poll to select the District 13 House candidate. I won and avoided a primary."

LEONARD CAMPBELL

"He was a fair man and a most interesting one. He kept current on not only what was happening in his own party but in Denver, Colorado and the country. After the reapportionment was finalized, we spent many hours together at Cherry Hills (Country Club) talking and playing golf."

CONNIE DINER

"I treasure having known him and having his friendship. He was the most completely loyal person I have ever known."

BRUCE DINES

"Bob had an unbelievable ability to build a team of dedicated followers and workers – even those who weren't always on his side of the fence. He truly had a heart of gold, but no patience for incompetence or mediocrity. I remember when I was County Treasurer and I discovered a discrepancy in the books due to a heavy hand from a paid employee. Bobby and I met late that night to go over the checkbook which had been locked in an old wooden desk of the employee. Bobby simply went to his car, returning with the tire jack handle and proceeded to pry the desk open – drawer by drawer, totally ruining the desk. After proving the discrepancy, Bob left a note to the employee on the front door to the office and we proceeded to place the remnants of the desk in the trash. Of course, the employee was gone forever the next morning."

TERRY GILBERTO

"He was a Goldwater Republican, an advocate of limited government, lower taxes, that sort of thing. He was always trying to improve the Republican Party. Not just this year or last year but always. He took his own polls by getting on the telephone and talking with people; or just riding in a taxicab and talking with the driver. Bob had a sixth sense for what was going to happen because of his conversations with anybody and everybody."

HELEN JOHNSON

"Many times in the past, I used to say to Bob, 'You ought to write a book,' and his reply was, 'Helen, if I did, half the population of Denver would have to move out of town.' He was such a great leader. When you left one of his Captain's meetings, you felt like waving the American flag and marching off to some invisible war! But he was also a very caring, compassionate person, especially when it came to animals."

NEIL JONES

"Bob was always recruiting candidates. Byron Rogers had been Denver's Congressman for years and nobody wanted to run against him. Bob called a meeting of the Captains; asked us to put names in the hat of potential candidates. I put my brother's name in the hat. Glenn had been wanting to run for something and was willing to make a long shot run against Rogers. Bob and the Captains agreed on supporting him. It was 1964 and Bob was concentrating on

Goldwater for President. Glenn gave it a go but it was not to be. After being defeated, he turned his attention to Cable TV which turned out to be more profitable."

RICHARD KIRK

"Bob Lee gave me my first introduction (to politics) and I learned a great deal from him. In 1958, I was appointed by Bob to be an area representative, coordinating three districts. Later he appointed me treasurer of the Denver County GOP. We often supported different candidates but Bob was hard to beat."

HERB KOETHER

"In a little over 40 years as a volunteer political activist, the one person who had the most influence on me, provided the most inspiration, knowledge and guidance, was Bob Lee. He knew more about building good government through the election of qualified people than anybody I ever met or heard of."

SAM LUSKY

"Technically, he was a politician, one of the best, skilled in strategy and attraction of others like him to the Republican Party. But his manner was anything but secretive or devious. He was an open faced Kansan with a ready wit, accompanied by a crinkly smile and a hearty chuckle. In all probability, Colorado will never produce another participant in politics who retained so successfully his sense of humor, his sense of values and his sense of balance."

BILL MYRICK

"Bob was always steadfast in his strict principles as to the type of campaign which must be conducted. He was always honest and forceful, but fair. He certainly was the first one that I can recall claiming the philosophy and the commitment of all candidates to the principle that 'I shall not speak ill of another Republican.'"

JIM NICHOLSON

"Bob Lee set the standard for political operatives. He was a superior strategist and exacting technician. He ran campaigns as a fine art. And it all started with his premise that a candidate had to earn each vote, one at a time."

WILL F. NICHOLSON, JR.

"I probably discovered John Love. I knew the Maytags in Colorado Springs and John performed some legal work for them. They held him in high regard. They told me John was interested in running for Governor. I called Bob and said I would meet him at Shaner's Restaurant in Downtown Denver to give him a candidate. Bob brought Ralph with him; we met and I told them about John. Bob and Ralph listened and the next thing I knew, John was the Republican candidate taking on Steve McNichols."

BOB ROSENHEIM

"I suggested to Bob on several occasions that he should be compensated for at least part of the time he was spending as Denver County Chairman. I knew he was having a difficult time financially and that I would raise the money. He would have no time for my suggestions. He said he was not in it (politics) for money; just good government – like the rest of us volunteers."

BOB ROLANDER

"Bob was the greatest person I ever met on the telephone. He could make 200 calls a day and get results. This was why he was such a fabulous recruiter."

BOBBIE RUSSELL

"I joined the Young Republicans in 1958 and was very active for Nixon in 1960 and Love in 1962. I was running for Young Republican State Chairman in 1963. Convention was in Estes Park. I was having trouble with the Denver delegates. I called Lee late at night and he and Ralph came up to Estes Park in the middle of the night to campaign for me. I lost to Don Smith but I will never forget their help."

ERIC SCHMIDT

"I decided to seek the nomination for House District 42 in Boulder County. I called Bob for advice. Bob wanted to be sure the

County leadership was behind me. I won on the first ballot against three others. Bob then gave me a handwritten seven page campaign organization format and said, 'Do this and you'll win.' Bob's approach was to analyze the District block by block and recruit a volunteer for every 20 houses. We won 9,439 to 6,936. All Bob said after the election was 'you did a good job. I told you you'd win.'"

JEFF SHOEMAKER

"The only aspect of life Bob cherished more than politics was his family. His greatest advice to me, more important than his advice on block workers, was to 'remember that being a good husband and father is far more important than any campaign.'"

FRANK SOUTHWORTH

"Republican, patriot, coach; Republican, golfer, tennis player; Republican, gin player, county chairman; Republican, campaign manager, smoker; Republican, thinker, Dad, husband; Republican, political engineer, organizer; Republican, American, FRIEND!"

CHUCK TAYLOR

"Bob was a man of his word. During the 1962 election, Adams County was running out of money so we worked a deal to borrow $5,000 and Bob said that whatever shortage we had in paying back, he would see that the amount was paid, and so he did. I did find out that in a Gin game he never was one to lose. He could count points as fast as he could count votes."

WELLINGTON WEBB

"My first real encounter with Bob was as a member of the Reapportionment Commission. During that time period I made it a point to sit between Bob and Bev Bledsoe. One day Bob asked me why I always made it a point to sit next to him. I told him that I knew he and Bev were older, wiser, more experienced, and eventually (would) try to trick me. I told him that I wanted to learn all of their tricks of the trade so that I could use them and one day pass them on."

EPILOGUE

Joe Shoemaker

This book should have been written by Robert E. Lee, and perhaps it would have been if his health had not deteriorated.

Bob talked about a book with me and others often before his death on July 3, 1998. He wanted to document his conservative Republican philosophy and the work he accomplished in organizing political campaigns for candidates who espoused that philosophy.

It was not difficult for me to take on the task of writing a Bob Lee book. His family supports the idea as do his friends and colleagues. While I have had some experience in putting books together – *Budgeting Is the Answer* and *Returning the Platte to the People* and assisting my wife, Penny Dykstra Shoemaker in publishing her *Memories*, I knew I would have to have help from a good writer.

I contacted Bill Miller, who had been a reporter and editor for the Durango Herald Democrat, The Rocky Mountains News and Denver Post, before becoming Mayor Tom Currigan's Executive Officer in 1963. Later, Bill was hired by the Denver Water Department. He retired in 1991 after serving as General Manager of the Department for 12 years. I first met Bill when I was an Administrative Assistant to Mayor Batterton and knew that he was familiar with Denver and Colorado politics. He is a registered Democrat, but, like many others of that party, he knew Bob and the work that he had accomplished. Bill agreed to help.

Early on, we discussed how I would handle, in the book, my political relationship and personal friendship with Bob throughout my political career. We agreed to keep personal references out of the text but have me include in an epilogue, memories of my 40-year association with Bob.

It started in early 1959. I was walking along a third floor hallway of the City and County Building in Denver in February of that year, headed for a court appearance for a client of a firm I was associated with, Holland and Hart, when a stranger stopped me. This gentleman said he knew me because I had graduated from Annapolis and he, too, had attended the U. S. Naval Academy. This person was Richard Y. Batterton, Manager of Public Works under Mayor Nicholson.

"Joe," he said. "I'm going to run for Mayor because Mayor Nicholson is not going to seek reelection. Will you help me?" I said that I would but that I knew very little about politics. He explained that in Denver it was a non-partisan race but his strong support would come from the Republican Party. He added that many of his Public Works employees were Democrats and he thought they would also help him. He told me that a fellow by the name of Bob Lee was going to run his campaign and that Bob had set up campaign headquarters across the street from City Hall in the Zook Building.

On the way back to my office in the Equitable Building, I went over to the 5th floor of the Zook Building and located a small office that had a red, white and blue sign on the door saying "Batterton for Mayor." I knocked on the door and a gruff voice said, "Come in." The man behind the voice was sitting on a chair with his feet on the desk, a telephone at his ear, and smoking a cigarette, a position that I was to see Bob in many, many times throughout the years. He waved me to a chair and finished the telephone call that was requesting dollars for the Batterton campaign.

Before I said anything, Bob looked straight at me and said: "I know you. You're one of Ralph's guys and you're also a Navy guy. Right?"

I had been recruited by Ralph Clark in 1958 to help in upcoming political campaigns. Ralph, who was with the law firm of Law, Nagle and Clark, had offices in the Equitable Building where Holland and

Hart was located. I had met Ralph in 1957 since we lived close to each other in Southeast Denver and I would often ride to and from work with him, since my wife, Penny and I, had only one car.

When I told Bob I was willing to work in the Batterton campaign, he gave me a quick civic lesson on Denver politics and then gave me an assignment. He told me that while the Charter stipulated that the election would be non-partisan, this simply meant the candidates did not run with the Party label. But both parties selected candidates of like political persuasion and supported them.

Bob told me that Batterton was a Republican and that he had a plan to get him elected by going door to door in every precinct in Denver. He told me he had two captains in Southeast Denver who needed help, Vera Schneider and Leonard Davis.

"They're good Republicans but they don't have half the committeemen and committeewoman spots filled in District 35," Bob told me. "I want you to call on them and tell them I sent you to help them in every way and let them know you're not after their jobs, because you don't even live in their District. Also, tell them you will be helping the captains in District 34, Penny Griffin and Bob Arnold, as well as Bob Rosenheim and Betty Unfug, the captains in District 36."

Since I was a Naval Academy graduate and President of the Naval Academy Alumni in Colorado, Bob told me he expected me to recruit some "good old Navy boys" who would assist in the campaign.

He told me precisely what he wanted me to do: "Joe, I want you to work with the captains to get precinct leaders. Keep letting me know how you are doing because I'm turning over to you the registered voter lists in those districts. Hopefully, you can make calls during your free time hours.

"While you are recruiting people, I want you to work with the captains to get new and old precinct leaders to get a worker in each block in those precincts. You will know when you have a committed block worker when the individual agrees to put up a sign in his or her yard for Batterton and a bumper sticker on the family car. The Republican block workers will not only get Republicans in the area to turn out for Batterton but will talk to some of their Democratic neighbors to support Batterton."

Even though it was eight weeks until the May election, he told me to start holding as many afternoon coffees for Batterton as could be scheduled through the captains. Batterton was being opposed in his bid for Mayor by two well-known Democrats, Roland (Sonny) Mapelli and George Cavender. Both were City Councilmen and well known. Mapelli was from North Denver, a strong Democratic area, and Cavender was a labor leader and had the support of organized labor.

Lee was more concerned about Mapelli. Lee then told me what the strategy would be. He said to tell everyone what a good mayor Batterton would be but also tell them that "Sonny Mapelli is closely associated with former Councilman Eddy Mapel who has a casino in Las Vegas and for all we know, is associated with the Mafia who own and operate the gambling houses in Las Vegas."

He then gave me about three pounds of registered voter lists, said good-by and returned to his first love, the telephone, to continue his never ending quest for funds and workers.

On the way home that night riding with Ralph, I told him about my afternoon meeting with Lee. Ralph told me he was glad that I finally got to meet the General and learn first hand from him "how we're going to win this election and build a really good Republican organization."

The 1959 campaign went the way Lee had planned it. Mapelli came in third in the May election, resulting in a June runoff between Batterton and Cavender, which Batterton won 58,016 to 50,305.

After the election, Penny and I drove to Iowa with our two children, Jean, then age 7 and Jeff, then age 4, to visit our parents in Alton and Hawarden, Iowa. Much to my surprise, I received a telephone call from Batterton asking me to become his Administrative Assistant. I didn't know what an Administrative Assistant was, but Batterton explained that basically "he keeps complainers off my back." I told him I would think about it and call him the following day.

I then placed two calls – the first to Bob Lee, and the second to Steve Hart, my boss at Holland and Hart, and a Democrat. Lee told me he had given my Iowa number to Batterton and encouraged me to take the job, that it would be good for the Republican Party and I would have an opportunity to learn about government first hand.

After conferring with Hart, who assured me it would be one of the best experiences of my life, I called Mayor-Elect Batterton, my new boss, and told him that I would accept the job, but expected to stay with him only a year or so.

That year turned into three because after serving a time as Batterton's Administrative Assistant, he asked me to take the Cabinet position of Manager of Public Works, which, at that time, by Charter also was Deputy Mayor.

That was one of the happiest experiences of my life. I learned how the combined City and County government functioned in Denver, how the idea of non-partisan government worked in the city since the Charter set forth a civil service procedure in which employees were hired by merit and not through political connections. I found this to be true particularly of Public Works employees who have some of the more onerous jobs in city government – operating the sewer system, picking up trash, operating land fills and maintaining streets as well as overseeing the operation of Stapleton Airport.

I left that position to run for the State Senate from Denver in 1962, the year Bob Lee managed John Love's first successful campaign. Bob asked me and all other Republican candidates to use all of our resources to help elect John, which we did. I carried Denver first out of the eight candidates running for four Denver Senate seats at large and Love also carried Denver. I was reelected to the State Senate for four year terms again in 1968 and 1972.

I was in the early months of my first term in the Senate when I attended a meeting of Denver Republicans at the Shirley Savoy headquarters. Bob gave me two surprises at that meeting – first, he announced that he was giving up the Denver chairmanship. And second, to my embarrassment, because I had worked for Mayor Batterton, Bob told the assembled captains that I should run for Mayor because Dick Batterton could not be reelected. He explained that Batterton was unable to clean up the police scandal and was unwilling to get rid of his Safety Manager, a cabinet member who was the civilian head of the Police, Sheriff's and Fire Departments.

I told the assembled group and Bob that there was no way I could run for mayor because Dick Batterton had treated me fairly and I simply "could not bite the hand that had fed me."

During my first caucus in the State Senate in December, 1962, I asked Senator Harry Locke of Hartzel (Park County) to help me get appointed to the Joint Budget Committee. Locke was Chairman of that Committee and I became his colleague. I was privileged to serve on that Committee throughout my Senate career and was its Chairman in 1973-74 and again in 1975-76. It was this experience that led me to publish my first book, *Budgeting Is the Answer.*

Bob Lee was no stranger to the State House. He frequently visited members of the Legislature and several times stopped in the Joint Budget Committee Office to chat. He would always encourage me to stay the course of no tax increases, even in the bad financial year that occurred in 1975, when state revenues dropped precipitously and the JBC had to make immediate cuts in the just approved 1975-76 budget.

Even though in 1964 the Governor and the majority members of the JBC were of the same political party, it did not mean that we always agreed on the no tax issue. Many times we were at odds with the Governor and this did not help me when I decided to take on another political campaign.

In 1966, Bob encouraged me and I ran for Lieutenant Governor. At that time candidates for the Governor and Lieutenant Governor offices did not run as a team.

He insisted that I sit at a desk in our headquarters at the Park Lane Hotel and call every county chairman, vice chairman, and central committee member in each of the 63 counties. Then, he said, when I finished, I should start all over again. By following his instructions meticulously, I received the nomination with a unanimous vote at the State convention, even though by this time Bob had left the State to run Claude Kirk's successful campaign for Governor in Florida.

I ran a strong race in the general election, but lost to Mark Hogan by 8,163 votes. The final tally was 322,613 for Hogan and 314,460 for Shoemaker.

Everyone plays the "what if" game occasionally. Sometimes I wonder "what if" I had been elected Lieutenant Governor? Would I have run for Lieutenant Governor again in 1970 when Love won a third term? (That's when the Lieutenant Governor candidates for each party ran as a team for the first time.) Governor Love resigned near the end of his third term to become Energy Secretary in Washington and John Vanderhoof, his Lieutenant Governor, became Governor. What if . . .?

In any event, throughout my political career, Bob never once asked me for any kind of help in any area of city or state government. He continually encouraged me to do a good job.

As the 80's and 90's slipped away, Bob would keep me informed of candidates he supported. His involvement always centered on issues of cutting back government regulations and lowering, or at least not raising, taxes.

I particularly remember the day after Christmas in 1997 when I received a telephone call from Bob asking me to join him for a late breakfast at the Village Inn on South Colorado Boulevard. Bob brought with him files of newspaper clippings and letters from political people about the campaigns in which he had been involved. At this breakfast he also showed me Washburn College yearbooks and a picture of his Dad in his college football uniform and himself in his football uniform. He told me, as he had on previous occasions, that he had boxes of memorabilia stored in the basement of his townhouse.

After we parted, I called Jim Aspinwall and related the meeting and said I would prepare a book outline that might be of use to Bob. Jim expressed satisfaction with the idea and said he would deliver it to Bob since I had made it clear to Jim that I did not feel I had the time nor the experience to write the book myself.

The subject never came up again until shortly before Bob's death when he expressed to Frank Southworth the thought that no one would remember what he had accomplished. Frank told me about this and I called on Bob then to assure him I would try to write something with the help of a political writer. He was not feeling well but seemed to perk up after I told him that he would be remembered.

I never carried on a conversation with him again. I visited him in the hospital the afternoon before his death but he was not aware of my presence. Bee, his wife, confided in me that, despite his condition, she and son Eric were going to take him home shortly. They did. That night, he died at home July 3, 1998.

And so, the publishing of this book fulfills my pledge to Bob. Now others can share my memories of this great individual who truly made a difference in Republican politics at the city, state and national level.

And he made a difference in my life, also.

A quotation from a book about General Robert E. Lee by Frank Buchser applies equally to Colorado's Robert E. Lee:

> *"One cannot see and know this great soldier without loving him."*